Echoes of
KENTUCKY
BASKETBALL

Echoes of
KENTUCKY
BASKETBALL
The Greatest Stories Ever Told

Edited by Scott Stricklin

TRIUMPH
B O O K S

Library of Congress Cataloging-in-Publication Data

Echoes of Kentucky basketball : the greatest stories ever told / edited by Scott Stricklin.
    p. cm.
    Includes bibliographical references.
    ISBN-13: 978-1-57243-887-3
    ISBN-10: 1-57243-887-8
    1. Kentucky Wildcats (Basketball team)—History. 2. University of Kentucky—Basketball—History. I. Stricklin, Scott, 1970–

GV885.43.U53E24 2006
796.323'630976947—dc22

2006019382

This book is available in quantity at special discounts for your group or organization. For further information, contact:

Triumph Books
542 South Dearborn Street
Suite 750
Chicago, Illinois 60605
(312) 939-3330
Fax (312) 663-3557

Printed in U.S.A.
ISBN-13: 978-1-57243-887-3
ISBN-10: 1-57243-887-8
Design by Patricia Frey
All photos courtesy of AP/Wide World Photos; jersey photo courtesy of Peter Kuehl.

CONTENTS

Foreword *by Tubby Smith*   vii

Introduction   ix

Section I: *The Games*   1

Kentucky Defeats Baylor in NCAA Basketball
  Final at Garden
Hatton Knots First Extra Set on 47-Footer
No Tricks in UK Victory
Goose Leads Wildcats to Fifth NCAA Title
21 Years Later, Cats Stage Another Miracle
LSU's Winning Streak Floored at Kentucky
Kentucky Easily Beats Louisville, 65–44
Sky-High Kentucky Cuts Houston Down to Size
Oh, What a Night! UK 100, LSU 95
Wildcats Preserve Holy Roman Empire
Miracle of Mardi Gras Had Many Heroes
Wildcats' OT Thriller a Work of Heart
Pitino Finally Completes His Long Walk to an NCAA
  Championship
Duke-Kentucky II: A Sequel to Remember
Victory a Tribute to Coach and Team
It's Kentucky—Not Florida—That Looks Like Number
  One on This Night
Guard Powers Cats to Win Over Archrival

Section II: *The Teams*   53

Rupp's Cats Fiddle Away
Cheers, Tears, and Big Crowds as "Rupp's Runts"
    Come Back Home
Book on Kentucky: Only Title Page Is Flawed
Seniors Took the Despair Out of Climb from Oblivion
I Am Kentucky, and I Love Surprises
Kentucky Provides Shining Example

Section III: *The Players*   81

Beard Thinks, Eats, Lives Basketball
Even Rupp Says Issel May Be UK's Best Big Man
    since Spivey
Macy's Magic
The Comeback of Sam Bowie
The Frustration Ends for Beal
Cry of the Cat: A Day of Happy-ness for Walker
Chapman, Basketball Inseparable
Mash Bash

Section IV: *The Coaches*   117

A Freshman Helps Hire UK Coach, Then Plays for Him
His Old Kentucky Home
From Old Kaintuck
No Tears, No Nostalgia, Just "Eternal Thanks" from
    Adolph
Kentucky's Baron Still Holding Court
The Right Mixture of Love, Hate Kept Rupp on Top
In Shadows, He Worked beside Rupp
Hall's Light Touch Gives Kentucky Old Feeling
Hall's a Complex Man Who Upheld Tradition
Counted Down and Out, Kentucky Injected with
    New Life by Pitino
At Kentucky, Tradition Takes a Twist
Kentucky's Newton Has Come Full Circle
Firm Hands, Loving Hands

Section V: *The Phenomenon*   167

Bleeding UK Big Blue
UK Program Carries Weight of a State on Its Shoulders
In the Bluegrass State, They're Thoroughly Bred to
    Win, or Else
The War within the State

Notes   193

FOREWORD

As a coach I find myself constantly talking to my players about responsibility. Whether it's a class project away from the court or setting a good screen and blocking out for a rebound on the court, handling responsibilities is an important part of the maturation process these young men go through while on the University of Kentucky campus.

One of those responsibilities we talk to our team about is the need to respect and carry on the great tradition of Kentucky basketball. They've heard about all the names—Rupp, Hall, Issel, Beard, Mashburn—and some of the great games. They look up at the rafters of Rupp Arena and see the banners recognizing the Final Four and national championship teams. Reminders of UK's past success are everywhere.

My hope is that our players understand how precious it is to wear those blue and white jerseys and to run out onto the Rupp Arena court in front of 24,000 fans. You see, when the Big Blue faithful cheer for the Wildcats, they aren't just supporting our current players, they are also celebrating the pride and history that Kentucky basketball represents.

This book touches on some of the legendary teams, players, and coaches who have made Kentucky basketball special. Their accomplishments set the standard that all future Wildcat teams are judged against. I'm honored to be a small part of that rich history, and in the years ahead I look forward to many more stories about great moments in Kentucky basketball.

—Tubby Smith

INTRODUCTION

To understand the allure of writing about Kentucky basketball, you must first understand the Wildcat fan base. Or, rather, the size of the Wildcat fan base.

Arguably no college program has the reach of Kentucky basketball. Starting in the Commonwealth of Kentucky, where more than 90 percent of the inhabitants who follow college sports claim an allegiance to the Wildcats, and branching out, UK fans settle over the basketball world like a dense fog in an eastern Kentucky holler. Their fanaticism overtakes the Southeastern Conference tournament each March, when Atlanta, Nashville, or New Orleans are re-branded "Cat-lanta," "Cats-ville," or "Big Blue Easy" because of the enormous numbers of Kentucky fans who invade those cities.

Those fans who aren't fortunate enough to have a ticket to a UK game help the Wildcats consistently deliver some of the largest television ratings, a phenomenon not missed by CBS, ESPN, and other networks. During the 2005–06 season, ESPN and ESPN2 televised 12 games involving SEC schools, six of which featured Kentucky. Those six Wildcat games were the highest-rated SEC games shown by ESPN. A late December nonconference game between Kentucky and Ohio doubled the rating of a January league matchup between Florida and Ole Miss.

Likewise, newspaper and magazine editors have understood for years that articles about the Big Blue drive readership in a way few things can. Ever since Adolph Rupp began producing wildly successful Kentucky teams in the 1930s, when he would take his group of Southern boys to New York and beat the big-city glamour teams of the time, columnists and sportswriters have been drawn to writing about the Wildcats.

I've enjoyed culling out some of the best writings about Kentucky from over the past few decades. Some of the early entries contain a style vastly different from what we read today, yet offer interesting historical perspectives on how Kentucky basketball was viewed a half century ago. The more modern selections tell about the personalities, dramas, and successes of the nation's winningest basketball program.

Although writing styles have changed over the years, the interest generated by these articles has remained constant, much like the fans' love of the Wildcats.

Head coach Rick Pitino (center) and daughter Jaclyn are surrounded by members of the team and media following Kentucky's win over Syracuse in the 1996 national championship game in East Rutherford, New Jersey.

Section I
THE GAMES

Louis Effrat, *The New York Times*

KENTUCKY DEFEATS BAYLOR IN NCAA BASKETBALL FINAL AT GARDEN

Much of Kentucky's early basketball reputation was built on the strength of wins in the Big Apple. The Wildcats won the 1948 national championship, their first, at New York's famed Madison Square Garden by defeating Baylor. Following is The New York Times' *account of that game.*

Kentucky's Wildcats, at no time in jeopardy, easily conquered Baylor, 58–42, last night at Madison Square Garden and romped to their first NCAA basketball championship. Off to an early 17-point lead, Adolph Rupp's powerhouse completely outclassed the Bears from Waco, Texas.

The second smaller turnout of the season, 16,174, witnessed this one-sided East-West final, in which Baylor's strategy—slowdown and stress possessions—succeeded only in holding down the score. Baylor, lightly regarded at the outset of the Western Regionals, qualified for the title clash with a pair of upset victories over Washington and Kansas State, but last night ran out of surprises.

Perhaps the best way to describe Kentucky's thirty-fourth and certainly most important triumph of the campaign is to report that form held up. Nearly every pregame prediction pointed to the size, speed, and depth of the Wildcats from Lexington and figured that these would determine the outcome. They did, too, even if Coach Rupp, who wanted to win this one above all others, saw little need to turn to his bench. He did not substitute until 6:30 of the second half, by which time the decision was just about clinched.

Alex Groza, the tallest man on the floor, was the high scorer for Kentucky and the game. His 14 points were two more than Ralph Beard tallied and four more than Bill Johnson made for Baylor. The

3

latter was unable to handle Groza's height, and most of the rebounds were dominated by the 6'7" center, who was voted the outstanding player of the tournament.

But Groza was far from being the only Wildcat in a starring role. Beard, an irrepressible digger; Ken Rollins, an all-around ace; Wallace "Wah Wah" Jones, a dependable workhorse; along with the steady Cliff Barker—all contributed handsomely toward a victorious cause.

That Baylor, because of Kentucky's height advantage, would resort to a deliberate style of attack, was anticipated. The Bears, reluctant to risk forfeiting possession, attempted to make certain that every shot was a clear one and from close range. As a result they had taken only one chance in the first four minutes and six in the first seven and a half, not one finding the target.

Thus Kentucky enjoyed a 13–1 spread—Jim Owen caged a foul shot at 5:25—and Baylor followers foresaw a rout.

Finally, when the clock showed seven minutes and 35 seconds gone, Don Heathington dribbled in with a layup, and the Texans, on their seventh attempt from the floor, achieved their initial basket.

However, this was not repeated often enough to lighten Baylor's burden, and at 12:35 Kentucky's lead was 17 points at 24–7. This shrunk slightly to 29–15 at the intermission, and later the Bears rallied to cut the deficit to nine points, but the Wildcats packed too many weapons and triumphed going away.

Kentucky, obviously superior in all departments, was most impressive during the early stages. One two-minute spurt netted seven points as Jones, Rollins, and Groza excelled.

The Wildcats were driving hard and harassing the Bears at every turn. Thereafter they performed commendably enough, but their rallies were intermittent and the Kentuckians did not again look that superb.

Probably the reason for this letup was lack of incentive. They were en route to victory and knew it, and no end of grimaces from Rupp on the bench sufficed to reawaken them. Baylor, on the other hand, did not have the power to take full advantage and suffered its sixth setback of the year.

In victory Kentucky attempted a total of 83 shots, clicking with 23, as compared to 15 out of 64 for the losers. Both teams automatically qualified for the Olympic trials, which get underway Saturday afternoon at the Garden.

Third place in the competition went to Holy Cross, despite an early 16-point lead, staggering to a 60–54 victory over Kansas State in the preliminary encounter.

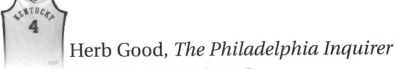

Herb Good, *The Philadelphia Inquirer*

HATTON KNOTS FIRST EXTRA SET ON 47-FOOTER

Vernon Hatton's 47-foot shot to force a second overtime against Temple is still noted by a star painted on the Memorial Coliseum floor. The Philadelphia Inquirer reported on the triple-overtime thriller in December 1957. UK would also down Temple later that season in the Final Four en route to its fourth NCAA title.

Vern Hatton, 6'3" senior University of Kentucky backcourtman, pulled victory out of Temple University's grasp by sinking a sensational 47-foot shot as the buzzer ended a five-minute overtime session tonight. But two additional extra periods were needed before Hatton finally was able to give the unbeaten Wildcats their third straight triumph, 85–83.

Hatton scored the last six Kentucky points of the third overtime period to tip the scales in a super-duper thriller that was filled with such suspense that one of the 12,300 [in attendance] died from the excitement before it was over. Even so, Temple's Mel Brodsky had a chance to extend the overtime but missed a short-side shot in the last furious seven seconds.

Ex-Commissioner Dies

William Baughn, former Lexington city commissioner, collapsed from a heart attack in the last 30 seconds of regulation play, which ended 65–65 when Hatton converted a free throw with 1:14 left and another with 49 seconds remaining to erase a 65–63 Temple lead.

Temple forged a 69–65 lead in the opening minutes of the first five-minute extra period only to have Kentucky rally for a tie at 69. However, when All-American Guy Rodgers, who helped pace the losers with 24 points, spun away from his guard and connected on a short jumper with three seconds left, it seemed certain Temple had the game in the bag.

But the never-say-die Wildcats called a timeout with one second left, just as they had done before time expired in regulation play. On that occasion, Adrian Smith, taking a throw-in at the center line from John Crigler, missed in a long, desperate heave.

Crowd Delirious

The second time Crigler put the ball into play, he threw it in to Hatton, about a step in front of the midcourt line. The latter got off a set shot the instant the ball reached his hands, and it arched its way 47 feet to the basket, as the buzzer sounded, and dropped cleanly through the hoop while the crowd went insane.

Temple went ahead in the second extra period at 73–72 on a rebound goal by Jay Norman at 2:37, but Ed Beck grabbed the rebound of Johnny Cox's missed free throw to regain the lead for Kentucky.

When Beck drew a foul against Rodgers with 55 seconds left, he not only cashed the first of two free throws to give the Wildcats a 75–73 lead but sent Rodgers to the sidelines with his fifth personal. The latter had been nursing four from 9:41 of the second half.

Brodsky ties at 75

But Temple wasn't finished. Brodsky converted two fouls with 53 seconds left to tie at 75–75, and the Owls got the ball back and worked Bill "Pickles" Kennedy free for a driving shot that just missed the mark as the second overtime ended.

Kennedy, who tallied 19 points in a tremendous all-around performance that more than upheld the high regard of Coach Harry Litwack, created the third tie (81–81) of the third overtime with a short jump shot with 1:53 to go, only to have Hatton break it for keeps with his second goal of the period at 1:40.

Twelve seconds later, Kennedy fouled out when he charged into Hatton on a drive, and the latter made his free throw and a bonus try to give Kentucky an 85–81 lead.

Still the scrappy Owls refused to admit defeat. They pulled within two when Brodsky, a brilliant 24-point performer, again converted two pressure fouls with 1:20 left. Temple still had a chance when Tink Van Patton got the rebound on Hatton's missed free throw with 24 seconds left, but Brodsky's last-ditch shot with seven seconds left skimmed off the rim. So when Kentucky's Beck came down with the rebound, it was all over.

The give-and-take of the overtime play was typical of the entire game. Temple enjoyed the biggest lead—eight points midway through the first half—but Kentucky cut it to 35–34 by the intermission, and from then on it was a wild scramble.

The Owls, who certainly didn't lose any stature from their first loss, tackle tough Cincinnati in the Ohio city Monday night before returning home.

Dave Kindred, *The* (Louisville) *Courier-Journal*

NO TRICKS IN
UK VICTORY

Prior to gaining national fame at The Washington Post *and* The Sporting News, *Dave Kindred served as sports editor of* The (Louisville) Courier-Journal. *Here he reports on Kentucky's upset win over previously undefeated Indiana in the 1975 NCAA Mideast Regional championship.*

A woman with a big smile and dancing eyes tapped Joe Hall on the shoulder. The University of Kentucky basketball coach was talking to reporters. "Can I interrupt the coach?" said Katharine Hall, who, as the coach's wife, knew the answer to that one.

Hall put his right arm around her, pulling her close, and they kissed on the basketball court at the University of Dayton Arena. Only minutes earlier, Kentucky had beaten Indiana 92–90 in a game full of cardiac arrests.

"Great, just *great*," Hall said into his wife's ear.

If Kentucky ever, in its rich history, played a more important game with more ferocity, someone will have to prove it to the 13,458 folks here.

By winning, UK is the NCAA's Mideast Regional champion and advances to the Final Four in San Diego. It will play Syracuse, champion of the East Regional.

By winning, UK ended Indiana's 34-game winning streak, handing the number one–ranked Hoosiers their first defeat of a remarkable season in which they performed with such precision that they dispatched opponents by an average of 23 points a game.

By winning, UK ended a melancholy streak of failure in the regional finals. Since Kentucky finished second in the 1966 NCAA tournament, it had lost four times in the regional championship game.

UK did it with straight basketball. No tricks. Not holding the ball. Lesser teams might have tried something crazy—especially a team that had lost to Indiana 98–74 on December 7, as UK had. Somebody asked Jimmy Dan Conner, a UK guard, if his team came into yesterday's game with trepidation.

"No," Conner said. "When we went out of the locker room to play, we were ANGRY. They beat us so bad the time before. We wanted to get 'em."

UK won because its guards, Mike Flynn and Conner, scored 39 points—18 over their combined average. And it won because its defense, aggressive and enthusiastic, broke Indiana's poise. Normally efficient and careful, Indiana was forced into 20 turnovers yesterday.

"They got that look on their faces that a coach likes to see in the opponents," Hall said.

What look?

"Like a look of wonder at what's happening."

It was, in fact, a wonder. People who make their living betting on sports events figured Indiana to win by 12 points. A Louisville sports editor (blush) said Indiana would win 93–81. He said UK could win only if Kevin Grevey, the star forward, scored 25 or 30. He said Indiana's Quinn Buckner would control Mike Flynn.

Wrong, wrong, wrong.

Flynn scored 22 points, nearly triple his average. He made six of six shots in the decisive second half. At game's end, they raised Flynn up last to give him the honor of cutting the last strand that held the net to the rim. Taking it in hand, Flynn shook it in the direction of Indiana rooters.

"I was thinking about all the times Indiana has beaten us, and all that stuff I've had to take back home," he said.

Flynn grew up in Jeffersonville. He was Indiana's "Mr. Basketball" in 1971. When he chose to play at Kentucky, and when Indiana beat Flynn and UK four straight times, the noise Jeff heard grew.

"They'd say, 'I told you, you should have gone to IU. They're winning, they're better than Kentucky.'

"And Indiana proved it. So what could I say? They had me."

Flynn sat at courtside, the net a necklace. He smiled. "Now maybe I can do some talking."

For Flynn, for Grevey, for Conner and Bob Guyette—for UK's senior starters— yesterday's victory was the stuff of dreams.

"I came to Kentucky to win a national championship and be All-America," Flynn said. "I won't be an All-American, but we still have a shot at the national championship."

Joe Hall recruited these seniors. While assistant to Adolph Rupp, Hall coached them as freshmen. He became boss the next year, and the four seasons have been full of drama.

"My freshman year, we were 22–0 and ranked number one in the country. We couldn't have asked for anything better," Flynn said. "As sophomores, we started out slow. A lot of things were going wrong. We had a lot of publicity, and there was a lot of pressure—and we weren't ready for it."

UK won 10 games in a row that year before losing to—yes— Indiana in the Mideast Regional championship game. The UK record was 20–8. Not bad most places, but at a school that has won four national championships, 20 victories is mediocre.

If 20–8 is mediocre, what is 13–13? "The downfall of our career," Flynn said of last season. "We let a lot of people down, and they started saying we weren't as good as we were supposed to be. We didn't live up to their expectations."

The problem, Flynn said, was one of manpower. "We just didn't have the big man. We had a small guard, two small forwards and no big man. That's changed now."

Any explanation of UK's turnaround—from 13–13 to 25–4 with two more victories needed for an NCAA championship—must begin with UK's two 6'10" freshman centers, Rick Robey and Mike Phillips.

Because they contributed so significantly and so quickly, Coach Hall could use the 6'9" Guyette at forward and the 6'4" Conner at guard. Suddenly, a small UK team was a very large one.

Robey brought more size. He is a fighter, and his aggressiveness rubbed off. If UK is anything, it is, to use a coaching word, "physical." That means it hits lots of people with lots of shoulders, elbows, and hips. Somebody asked Conner how UK handled Indiana's screening offense so well.

"Coach Hall decided that any illegal pick would be met with force," he said.

The game at times was a heavyweight fight. Bodies flew. Twice, fists flew. Guyette inadvertently decked Kent Benson, IU's 6'11" brute, with a forearm. Benson threw an elbow at Robey, connecting solidly— and it was at that moment, with 5 minutes and 32 seconds to play, that UK's season came full circle.

On December 7, Benson humiliated Robey, a seasoned and skilled sophomore overwhelming a freshman in his third college game. The humiliation included a forearm smash to the teeth. No foul was called.

A man sought out Robey after that game. Was the rookie frightened? Did he want to go home?

"I learned something today," Robey said. The big guy smiled. He was at ease. No big deal. "I'll put it to use."

So yesterday Robey scored 10 points (and Phillips had 10, too). Robey's last two came on free throws after Benson's deliberate foul, a maneuver he got away with December 7. The free throws gave UK a 79–70 lead, its biggest of the game until then.

UK held on to win. "It was 40 minutes of the most intense basketball I've ever seen," Conner said. When it was over, Katharine Hall kissed her husband, and outside the locker room an old woman with white hair kissed Steve Green, who had 21 points for the losers.

"I love you," the woman said. Green had tears in his eyes.

Paul Borden, *The* (Louisville) *Courier-Journal*

GOOSE LEADS WILDCATS TO FIFTH NCAA TITLE

Led by Final Four MVP Goose Givens, who exploded for 41 points against Duke in the title game, Kentucky gave Joe B. Hall his national championship in his sixth season as head coach. To national media types covering the event, UK's first crown in 20 years seemed to bring more relief than joy. Paul Borden covered the 1978 game for The *(Louisville)* Courier-Journal.

Kentucky can celebrate now. Jack "Goose" Givens, in the finest performance of his sparkling career and one of the best ever in NCAA championship game history, led the Wildcats to their fifth national title last night.

Kentucky's 94–88 victory over Duke in the final game of the 40th annual NCAA tournament climaxed a season of pressure in grand style for the darlings of the Bluegrass. "The pressure's been on six seasons, really," said Wildcat coach Joe B. Hall as he was mobbed by fans, reporters, and television crews on the floor of the Checkerdome afterward.

Hall, who took over for Adolph Rupp in 1972 and lived in the shadow of the legendary coach, had spoken of the pressures of coaching at Kentucky a day earlier. He said his team, ranked number one nearly every week of the season, had not taken time to enjoy any of its accomplishments—including a 31st Southeastern Conference crown—this year. It can now.

Givens, the number two all-time Kentucky scorer, put on a tremendous show before a steamy crowd of 18,721, scoring a career-high 41 points. He hit 18 of 27 from the floor in scoring the third highest total for an individual in the NCAA final. His final-game total is topped only by Bill Walton's 44 in 1973 and Gail Goodrich's 42 in 1965, both for UCLA.

"There's no finer way to go out," said Givens, who cut the last strand of the netting on the south basket to the cheers of the Kentucky throng. "I'm happy for the team and for the people of the state of Kentucky because they love basketball so much there."

Givens scored 16 of Kentucky's final 18 points in the first half, getting the Wildcats on top, 45–38, at the break. It was a whirlwind finish in the closing minutes of the first half that got Kentucky a fairly comfortable margin.

With 57 seconds left, Duke's Gene Banks, who played despite receiving a death threat before the game, hit two free throws to cut Kentucky's lead to 39–38.

The next trip down, Givens fumbled the ball in the lane but recovered to put in a jumper over 6'11" Mike Gminski, who missed from underneath at Duke's end.

Givens drilled one from the corner to get it up to 43–38 as the final seconds of the period ticked away. Duke rushed the ball down the floor, but Banks was called for charging—Givens, of course.

Givens went to the free throw line and hit both shots with three seconds left to put Kentucky on top by seven points.

"I was really ready," said Givens, "I never felt better before a game than I did tonight."

Duke, probably the youngest team ever to play in the final game, with a starting lineup of a junior, two sophomores, and two freshmen, hung tough, however, cutting Kentucky's lead to three in the opening minutes of the second period.

"Duke played an outstanding game," said Hall, "and we played super."

Kentucky, whose four seniors—Givens, Rick Robey, James Lee, and Mike Phillips—had played and lost to UCLA in the 1975 championship game, never faltered.

Lee got Kentucky its first basket of the second half with a hook, and after Duke's Jim Spanarkel got that basket back, Givens missed a jumper, Lee missed a follow-up shot, and Givens tipped it in.

Kentucky got a little more breathing room when Duke coach Bill Foster was called for a technical foul with 17:35 to go. Foster thought Kentucky's Truman Claytor had walked under the pressure in the backcourt, but all he got for his protests was the "T" from Big Ten referee Jim Bain.

Kyle Macy, as is his custom, made both free throws and then bounced a pass into Robey, who dunked one to give Kentucky a 55–46 lead. Kentucky stretched that margin to 12 points quickly at 60–48 and moved the lead up to 16 at 66–50 when Givens hit a follow shot and was fouled. Still, Duke refused to give in.

In fact, in the closing seconds, when Hall pulled his veterans from the game, Duke got the deficit down to 92–88 after Gminski hit a turn-around jumper. Duke called timeout with 10 seconds left to set up a press defense. But by then Kentucky's regulars were back in the game, and the Kentucky season ended in a most appropriate fashion.

A long pass went to Lee in the Kentucky forecourt, and the big senior from Lexington eluded Duke's Bob Bender and went in for a dunk that made the final margin six points.

Free throws kept Duke in the first period. Duke ran off a string of 12 straight and trailed only 21–20 when the teams went to the bench for a television timeout at 9:41. For the first period, Duke was 20-for-21 from the line and only 9-for-23 from the field—39.1 percent. Kentucky, meanwhile, was 18-for-34 form the field but went to the line only 12 times and hit nine.

Banks led Duke in scoring with 22 points followed by Spanarkel with 21 and Gminski with 20. After Givens's 41, Robey followed with 20 for Kentucky. Robey also had 11 rebounds to lead Kentucky. Gminski led Duke's rebounding with 12 as Duke enjoyed a 35–32 edge on the boards.

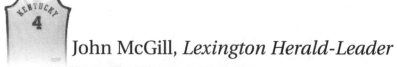

John McGill, *Lexington Herald-Leader*

21 YEARS LATER, CATS STAGE ANOTHER MIRACLE

Trailing by six points with 30 seconds left in overtime, freshman Dwight Anderson and senior Kyle Macy sparked a stunning Wildcat comeback over fifth-ranked Kansas in December 1978. The comeback was capped when the Jayhawks were called for a technical with three seconds left for trying to call a timeout they didn't have. In describing the scene, the Lexington Herald-Leader *referenced Vernon Hatton's miraculous shot against Temple 21 years earlier.*

December 7, 1957. One second on the clock and UK fans heading for the exits. Vern Hatton gets the inbounds pass, wheels, and shoots at the basket a mile away. Incredibly, the ball goes in, and Kentucky goes on to beat Temple in three overtimes. A miracle is born.

Vern Hatton stood unnoticed in Rupp Arena Saturday night, long after the pandemonium had ceased, long after Kentucky had added another miracle to its legend—strangely, almost 21 years to the day that Hatton launched his shot heard and since rehashed around the Commonwealth.

The Wildcats upset fifth-ranked Kansas in overtime, 67–66, after being behind 66–60 with less than 30 seconds to play.

"They can forget all about me now," smiled Hatton, "and talk about this one for the next 20 years."

They just might. Until the final score, Kentucky had never led in this game since a 10–8 advantage in the first minutes. And when KU sophomore Darnell Valentine's two free throws made it 66–60 with 31 seconds on the clock, many of the 23,472 fans in Rupp Arena headed for the cold, icy outdoors, unaware of the hot, hectic events upcoming.

Was Hatton among them?

"Almost," he said, grinning. "No, not really. Ever since that Temple game, I don't leave my seat anymore until a game's over."

It wasn't over, thanks to a spectacular half-minute by Kentucky freshman Dwight Anderson and clutch shooting by the old vet, Kyle Macy.

With 22 seconds left, Anderson drove the lane for a basket that trimmed the Kansas lead to 66–62. Valentine then was called for a foul on the inbounds pass. Anderson missed the free throw, but in some wild battling on the boards, he got the ball and was fouled again. This time, with 10 seconds left, he hit both free throws. Kansas 66, UK 64.

Then things really got wild.

Kansas called timeout—its last one of the game, and it proved critical—and UK coach Joe B. Hall told his team to try for a steal, hope for a charging foul, and—if worse came to worse—foul.

On the inbounds pass, Anderson batted at the ball, then leaped into the UK bench in an attempt to get it. In midair, his back to the court, he got the ball and heaved it, all with one hand. The ball floated halfway between midcourt and the UK foul line. Macy grabbed it, stopped from 15, and shot.

Swish. The crowd's roar preceded the scoreboard's incredible message: Kentucky 66, Kansas 66. Three seconds left. Moments later, the roar grew even louder. Despite having exhausted its timeouts, Kansas had yelled for time. A technical was called. When it was announced on the PA, hysteria reigned. Anderson dropped to his knees and clenched his fists in joy. And Macy prepared to shoot the technical.

Macy launched the free throw, which appeared off. He danced along the foul line as the ball danced along the rim. It dropped, UK led 67–66, and that's how it stayed as the Cats inbounded from midcourt and let the clock run down.

"It was really exciting to be out there," said Macy in an understatement that brought laughter from the press crunched around him.

Kansas coach Ted Owen, whose team lost for the first time in five outings, was in anything but a laughing mood. In a terse, quiet tone, he said, "We made some mistakes at the last, but when we were ahead by six with 31 seconds to go, the officials eased up. They had called a fine game up to that point. [UK's Clarence] Tillman obviously charged, but no foul was called.

"On Kentucky's next possession, [LaVon] Williams was on the rim but nothing was called. If they had continued to call the game the way they had earlier, we would have won.

"These boys deserved to win. It was an absolute crime they didn't. That's all I have to say."

Ironically, UK coach Joe Hall hadn't been too happy with the refs through the first 44½ minutes. "I'm not going to say anything about the officials," he told one bystander, "but I hope somebody does."

Hall was particularly perturbed in the last moments of regulation when twice Chuck Aleksinas was called for walking in the lane when UK needed a basket to tie the score.

Macy took care of the Cats' long struggle to come back, however, when he took the dribble away from Tony Guy and shot downcourt for a layup to make it 56–56 with 2:43 left in regulation.

Kansas, which often used a four-corner offense, went to it again and stalled. Truman Claytor's excellent defensive play forced a jump ball with Valentine with 52 seconds left, but Kansas got the tip. With 19 seconds left, the Jayhawks called time and plotted for a final shot by Valentine. He took it with two seconds showing, but the shot from the right of the key hit the side of the rim. Overtime.

It could, of course, be argued that both teams deserved to win this one. Valentine would appear to deserve a better fate, what with 27 points, four assists, and six rebounds.

Yet it was Valentine who made some crucial turnovers late in regulation play and in the overtime. He had eight turnovers in all. Despite that, his speed and savvy provided UK fans with one of the best performances by a guard in many a game.

"He's very tough, a very good player," said Hall. "But we have some tough ones, too."

Kentucky refused to fold all night—despite hitting just 38.7 percent in the first half against a KU zone that had them struggling, despite being behind 34–24 in the first half, down nine early in the second half, and behind 51–44 with 8:19 left in regulation.

Macy, still troubled by an injured thigh, was on the bench for almost the first 10 minutes of the second half. He wound up UK's leading scorer, however, with 15 points, and led in assists with four.

Jay Shidler, voted UK's most valuable sub (this before Anderson's heroics), had eight points. Consecutive long bombs by Shidler and Macy cut a Kansas lead of seven to 51–48. Moments later, Shidler's 15-footer and Aleksinas's lane shot cut it to 55–54.

Badly outrebounded in the first half (21–10), UK was much more aggressive after that. LaVon Williams led the effort with nine rebounds and Fred Cowan added seven as UK trimmed the final board margin to three, 32–29. Kansas was led by 7'2" Paul Mokeski with eight grabs.

Hall's young team has a surprising 3–0 record now, with old rival Indiana awaiting it next Saturday. There was little time to think about that game in the celebration following this miracle, however. In fact, Hall had jokes on his mind more than IU.

"That technical at the end wasn't that all important," he said. "We would have stolen the inbounds pass, anyway."

Vern Hatton would probably agree. It was, after all, a night for another miracle.

Ron Rapoport, *Chicago Sun-Times*

LSU'S WINNING STREAK FLOORED AT KENTUCKY

LSU brought a number-two ranking and a perfect 17–0 Southeastern Conference record into Rupp Arena for the Wildcats' senior day in 1981. The Bayou Bengals were greeted by a then-record crowd of 24,011 and a Kentucky team determined to get revenge for a 14-point loss earlier in the season in Baton Rouge. As is so often the case when top-ranked foes visit Lexington, national newspapers, such as the Chicago Sun-Times *in this instance, decide to send someone to report on the action.*

The game didn't mean a thing.

It didn't mean the Southeastern Conference championship. Louisiana State had that wrapped up a week ago.

It didn't mean NCAA tournament berths. Bringing in records of 27–1 and 21–4, respectively, LSU and Kentucky already were assured of that.

It didn't even mean a running start going into the NCAA playoff. With the SEC tournament coming up next week, these two teams might well have to do it all over again.

But when it was over, it would have been hard to find anyone in Rupp Arena Sunday who was indifferent to the outcome.

Blocked Shot Saved It

Here was Kentucky center Sam Bowie bounding across the key to block Howard Carter's final shot with four seconds remaining to preserve a 73–71 victory and break LSU's 26-game win streak.

There was the record crowd of 24,011 howling with glee at the final play while Carter picked himself up off the floor, looked at a referee, and hoped for a foul call that didn't come.

And there was Kentucky coach Joe B. Hall being carried off the floor by his players as if it were another national title for the Wildcats.

"We were embarrassed at LSU," Bowie said of Kentucky's 81–67 loss this season. Not to mention the thought of being part of a

Kentucky team that was entering its own arena an underdog for one of the few times since the invention of bourbon and branch water.

Longest Streak Ended

The end to LSU's streak, which was the longest in the nation and was posted by a team that is becoming the closest thing there is to a consensus choice to win the NCAA title, came like this:

After nearly losing the ball three times in the game's final minute, LSU took the ball out of bounds under the Kentucky basket with 10 seconds remaining.

Howard Carter threw it in to Ethan Martin deep in the forecourt. Everybody on both teams knew where the ball was going next—back to Carter, the deadliest outside shooter on the floor and the day's scoring leader with 24 points.

"We knew he was the man for the money," said Bowie. "We thought he would shoot from 20 feet."

So did Carter. After Martin threw him the ball in the corner, he was setting up behind Rudy Macklin's pick when he saw a hint of daylight and decided to try to improve his position.

"I saw the baseline open and I went in," Carter said. "I was hoping to draw the foul or get the basket."

What he got was most of Bowie's 7'1" frame in his face and every place else. Bowie knocked Carter's shot skittering over to Kentucky guard Dirk Minniefield, who dribbled out the clock and put Carter on the floor.

"He touched me," the LSU guard said. "I didn't fall on the floor myself. But I don't know if it was enough for a foul. If I would have been a spectator, I could tell."

Peter Alfano, *The New York Times*

KENTUCKY EASILY BEATS LOUISVILLE, 65–44

It's almost hard to imagine a time when Kentucky and Louisville didn't play annually on the hardwood, but it wasn't until this game in November 1983 that the game became a regular part of the common-wealth's schedule. The New York Times *ran this story about how the Wildcats avenged an overtime loss to Louisville in the 1983 NCAA Mideast Regional final by routing the Cardinals in Rupp Arena.*

For the time being, blue and white have been reaffirmed as the commonwealth's official colors, and the best team resides in what many basketball fans believe is its rightful place, Lexington. But in the rush of excitement following Kentucky's convincing 65–44 victory over Louisville tonight, it was the players who cautioned against anyone making too much of what was only the first game of a season that is long enough to allow Louisville ample time to recover.

"I don't go in much for statistics," said Jim Master, the Kentucky guard who led all scorers with 19 points. "Louisville lost some players, and maybe playing in a big place like this intimidated them. But they'll be great in March."

Master wasn't merely being magnanimous in victory. Past performances show that Louisville usually is a slow-starting team that peaks by the time the National Collegiate Athletic Association tournament begins. "We didn't execute much of anything well tonight," said the Cardinals coach Denny Crum, "but the national championship is won in April, not November."

Still, Kentucky's performance was impressive in the first regular-season meeting between the schools in 61 years. They have played on four occasions in postseason tournaments, most recently last spring when Louisville won, 80–68, in overtime in the Mideast Regionals. That game finally convinced the athletic board at Kentucky to authorize a renewal of the series against Louisville, despite the objections of the athletics director, Cliff Hagan, and Coach Joe B. Hall.

Once the game became a reality, however, Kentucky insisted that it be played early to keep the anticipation from building throughout the regular season. Hall had said all week that this would be treated as just another opening game, although no one really believed him.

"But there was a funny atmosphere the whole day today," said Sam Bowie, the 7'1" forward who returned to action after missing the last two seasons with a stress fracture of the left shin. "We were really loose. Even the coaches were loose, and you usually can tell when Coach Hall is getting ready for a big game. But he never said, 'This is it. We have to win.'"

So a feeling of camaraderie existed before the start of the game when the Louisville and Kentucky cheerleaders clasped hands at mid-court and gently swayed as the crowd sang "My Old Kentucky Home." Players on both teams exchanged handshakes and small talk. Oddly enough, only two of the players who started tonight's game are from Kentucky.

Limit on Hospitality

The Wildcats, however, put a limit on their hospitality. With more than 24,000 fans cheering and waving blue and white pompons, the Wildcats broke open a close game midway in the first half, outscoring Louisville 7–0 and 13–0 to take a 35–20 lead. Master found the range with his jump shot, and Melvin Turpin, the aggressive 6'11" center, was too big and formidable for the smaller Cardinals under the basket.

But the most intriguing aspect of the game was the role played by Bowie, who looked like the tallest point guard in the country. Bowie's accurate passes to Turpin and the other forward, Kenny Walker, enabled them to score several easy baskets.

And when Louisville tried to disrupt Kentucky with its renowned full-court press, Bowie helped neutralize it as the Kentucky guards lobbed their inbounds passes to him. Bowie had five assists, five blocked shots, and 10 rebounds. He had just seven points, all from the free throw line.

"There aren't too many big men who are willing to make the sacrifice that I am," he said. "But I'm pleased with the role I'm playing because my teammates appreciate it. Me and the other guys on this team came out of high school accustomed to scoring 30 points a night."

Kentucky's height advantage was crucial even though Louisville outrebounded the Wildcats, 41–36. But with Bowie and Turpin camped under the basket, the guards Lancaster Gordon and Milt Wagner—the focus of the Cardinals offense—could not penetrate as they had hoped. And their outside shooting was poor. They combined to score only 12 points.

Thus, Kentucky had made a rout of the game early in the second half, leading at one time by 29 points, 55–26, before coasting to the victory. "It didn't prove anything," Master said, "although deep down, it would have been tough to face some people if we had lost."

Fred Mitchell, *Chicago Tribune*

SKY-HIGH KENTUCKY CUTS HOUSTON DOWN TO SIZE

This rare regular-season matchup of eventual Final Four participants featured seven-footers Melvin Turpin and Sam Bowie of Kentucky and Akeem Abdul Olajuwon of Houston. Both teams had their seasons ended by eventual national champion Georgetown; Kentucky's in the national semifinal and Houston in the title game. Following is the Chicago Tribune's *game story.*

The glass backboards were covered with fingerprints, more than circumstantial evidence that Sunday afternoon's game between national powers Kentucky and Houston was played above the rim.

The Wildcats, with their two seven-footers—Melvin Turpin and Sam Bowie—dangling from the Rupp Arena rafters, outhammered the Cougars and 7' shot-blocking specialist Akeem Abdul Olajuwon, 74–67, in front of 23,992 fans.

"I'm not looking forward to going up against Akeem again in the [NCAA] tournament," Bowie said. "We're just glad to get this one out of the way."

Turpin scored 19 points, pulled down 11 rebounds, and blocked two shots. Bowie, in his best effort since coming back from two years of leg injuries, scored eight points, grabbed 18 rebounds, and blocked a pair of shots. Olajuwon scored 14 points, took down 12 rebounds, and rejected five shots before fouling out with 6:14 left in the game.

"I would like to play these guys again on a neutral floor," complained Olajuwon, whose team fell to 16–3. "Everything I do, they [the officials] call me for everything. I should be used to it by now, but the Kentucky players, they just jumped into me and the refs called me for the fouls."

Houston stormed to early leads of 7–0 and 11–1, forcing turnovers and missed shots with an aggressive, trapping defense.

"Houston came here to work immediately. They weren't intimidated by the 24,000 fans," said Kentucky sophomore forward Kenny Walker, who led the Wildcats' scoring with 20 points. "Obviously, their objective was to take the crowd out of the game right away."

With the score 11–1, Kentucky coach Joe B. Hall called a timeout and replaced overanxious freshman guard James Blackmon with steady sophomore Roger Harden. With Harden's court direction, Kentucky (14–2) began its slow uphill battle that earned the Wildcats a 35–31 halftime lead.

"I just wanted to get these guys organized. I just did my job," said Harden, a product of Valparaiso [Indiana] High School. "I thought maybe I had gone back to high school because I felt so free out there today."

The outstanding array of individual talent on the floor was evidenced by the 25-point performance of Houston guard Alvin Franklin (19 in the second half) and the 19-point, nine-rebound job of Michael Young.

But the ominous presence in the middle of Kentucky's Bowie and Turpin and Houston's Olajuwon helped force erratic shooting and poor execution. The Wildcats were guilty of 24 turnovers. Houston made only 34.7 percent of its shots from the field (26 of 75).

"We didn't win this game by execution," Hall said. "We won this one on emotion."

Kentucky stretched its lead to 61–51 with 7:56 to play on a Walker jam after a Harden alley-oop. Following a timeout, Houston cut the deficit to 62–59 behind Franklin and Young.

Hall ordered his Wildcats to spread out the offense in the final 3:16, but it almost backfired. Franklin ran off six straight points—two free throws, a pull-up jumper, and a steal and layup. That made the score 70–67 with 1:55 left.

"We had a chance to win until about 40 seconds were left," Houston's Guy Lewis said. "I would rather have had an 11–1 lead toward the end of the game than at the start."

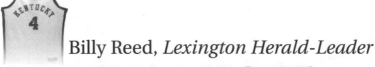

Billy Reed, *Lexington Herald-Leader*

OH, WHAT A NIGHT! UK 100, LSU 95

LSU's Dale Brown had amassed a spectacular array of talent for the 1990 season, featuring future pros Chris Jackson and Shaquille O'Neal. Kentucky, meanwhile, was in the first year under Rick Pitino and in the first year of a two-year NCAA postseason ban. The undermanned Cats finished the season 14–14, but didn't lose a home SEC game and, as Herald-Leader *columnist Billy Reed points out, earned the commonwealth's admiration for their gritty and fearless play.*

They already had earned a special place in the hearts of Kentucky basketball fans everywhere, so they really didn't *have* to beat big, bad Louisiana State last night before a record crowd in Rupp Arena.

But the fact that they did, withstanding a spectacular second-half shooting performance by LSU's amazing Chris Jackson, gave them all a night they can always hold dear and cherish as long as they live.

The score was UK 100, LSU 95 in what was merely an unbelievably exciting game. Ask any of the 24,301 who were there, some of whom reportedly paid upwards of $100 for a ticket. After blowing out to a 23-point lead, the Cats let LSU cut it to only two, 94–92, on a Jackson three-pointer, this one from somewhere deep in Jessamine County, with 1:12 to play.

At this point the Cats were reeling; so enormous had been their effort, but they weren't about to let it get away. Richie Farmer saw to that. Under the most intense pressure imaginable, the pride of Clay County knocked down six straight free throws in the final moments, in addition to coming up with a loose ball on an LSU possession.

At the end, after a final three-pointer effort by Jackson had missed, Farmer came up with the loose ball with only a couple of seconds remaining and held up an index finger to signify who was number one on this emotion-charged night when UK legends Adolph Rupp, Joe B. Hall, Dan Issel, and Cotton Nash were recognized.

And that was the signal for the crowd to finally release the emotion that had lifted and carried this team all night, beginning with the pregame warm-ups. The ensuing roar, an explosion of joy, was the ultimate tribute to this team that has worked so hard and come so incredibly far.

"My esteem for this team can go no higher," said Coach Rick Pitino, the miracle worker from New York. "This is an amazing bunch of guys. I told them at halftime, 'You don't want this game to ever end.' These moments in basketball are so few and so far between."

Especially for a team of which so little was expected before the season.

Reeling from the widely publicized NCAA probation and possessed of less natural talent than any Wildcat team since the Great Depression, this team has scuffled and hustled and clawed its way to a season that is downright amazing.

On October 15, a man could have gotten himself committed for predicting that the Wildcats would be where they are today. The record is 13–10.

The team is only a half-game off the Southeastern Conference lead. There is a fighting chance for a winning season.

How can this be? How can these scrawny UK players manage to beat the most talented and intimidating LSU team that Dale Brown has ever brought to Lexington? How can guys like Farmer and Sean Woods and Deron Feldhaus hold their own against all that beef and ability?

Simple, really. It begins with Pitino, who demanded conditioning and instilled confidence. The players do the rest. They play smart, they play hard, they create chaos, and they never quit. Mostly, they dare to dream.

"This is one of the biggest moments in my life," Farmer said. "I'm just so glad we won it. LSU is a good team, and Chris Jackson is just tremendous."

As Pitino pointed out, last night's game amounted to UK's NCAA tournament, considering that the Wildcats are barred from postseason play, and the atmosphere was worthy of any game that will be played any time in March.

It's too bad it couldn't be televised, because nowhere—Big East, Big Ten, Big 8, take your pick—has there been a better crowd or more emotion, and UK pulled all the stops to tap it.

The arena was festooned with all sorts of homemade banners and signs.

Besides the usual stuff such as "LS-Who" and "Gaux Home, Tigers," there was a decided fight motif ("Cats KO Tigers in Round 2") as a result of the celebrated Pitino-Brown tiff during LSU's 94–81 victory in Baton Rouge.

Tony Leonard, the noted equine photographer, was tapped to sing the national anthem, and all you stats nuts should know that UK is unbeaten in games where Leonard does his animated version of "The Star-Spangled Banner."

Last night, even before Leonard could get to the bit about the land of the free and the home of the brave, the record crowd was shrieking.

Then came a special ceremony in which UK athletics director C.M. Newton went to midcourt and announced the retirement of jerseys in honor of former Wildcat coaches Rupp and Hall.

Since Rupp never wore a UK jersey—he played his college ball for Kansas—the university might have been better served by hanging one of his trademark brown suits up there with the jerseys of the immortals who played for the Baron in his 42-year career.

As for Hall, he received an ovation unlike any he ever got in his 13 years as Rupp's successor. Walking off the floor, Hall paused to shake hands with Pitino and each of the players.

While the emotion on the UK bench was obvious, LSU and the volatile Brown seemed unusually subdued in the early going, when the Tigers' offense consisted mostly of Jackson firing at will from the outside and the big guys, most notably seven-footers Shaquille O'Neal and Stanley Roberts, crashing the boards.

When the Wildcats pushed the lead into double figures and then all the way up to 23, a blowout seemed possible. But the young Tigers, to their credit, kept their poise and cut it to 48–36 at halftime.

The second half was a war of attrition, with the main question being whether UK would be able to withstand the constant assaults led by Jackson. Of his game-high 41 points, 26 came in the second half.

"I've never seen a guy have a game like that, except maybe for Michael Jordan one night in the NBA," Pitino said. "We had two or three guys chasing him, and he just kept making threes. I don't think we could have hit the rim off the three's he was taking. That was a spectacular performance, but the amazing thing is, we still won the game."

They did, indeed. And in the process, they gave themselves and their fans a victory that will be remembered long after the players are old and gray and only distant memories.

Frederick C. Klein, *The Wall Street Journal*

WILDCATS PRESERVE HOLY ROMAN EMPIRE

The Wall Street Journal *used the 1991 Kentucky-Louisville matchup as a backdrop to describe the renaissance taking place in Lexington under second-year head coach Rick Pitino. The Wildcats' 103 points was the first time either team had cracked the century mark against their rival.*

They take their college basketball seriously in this home city of the University of Kentucky. Just how seriously came through to me Saturday evening while I was waiting for an elevator at the Hyatt Hotel here. The hotel is next door to Rupp Arena, where Kentucky soon would play its in-state rival, the University of Louisville.

Waiting with me was a boy nine or 10 years old and an adult who I assumed was his father. Both were obviously game-bound and wearing blue sweaters bearing the huge, white Kentucky "K."

"Who're you rooting for?" I asked the kid, teasingly.

"The Roman Empire!" he exclaimed, as Dad nodded approvingly.

The grandiosity of the kid's reply took the wind out of me, so I didn't remind him of what finally happened to the real Roman Empire. But if I had, he'd probably have told me that it lasted 500 years.

Kentucky hasn't been on top of the college hoops heap for quite 500 years, but it sometimes seems that way. Kentucky teams won national titles for "Baron" Adolph Rupp when basketballs had laces, and at various times since. Anything less than a 30-win season and the state legislature calls for an investigation.

I asked around and was told that people hereabouts are semi-serious about that "Roman Empire" stuff. I could have deduced as much from UK's basketball media guide. According to this remarkable document, Kentucky doesn't just have coaches, it has coaching "eras." This is the third season RPE. That stands for Rick Pitino Era.

Pitino's Wildcats were 14–14 in the won-lost column in his first year and 22–6 last season. To say that expectations are high for this campaign would be to put it mildly. "The heat is on" for 1991–92, declares—yes—the media guide. "The past two years have been fun, but everyone's saying your honeymoon is over," the coach is reminded elsewhere in this publication of the university that employs him.

In truth, 22–6 in just two seasons might have seemed unattainable anywhere but here when Pitino, now 38 years old, arrived. The Roman Empire was looking holey at the time as a result of a probation visited upon it by the NCAA. After years of giving off enough smoke to cure every ham in the South, UK basketball came to grief when a package bound for a recruit's parent mysteriously came apart in an express-mail office and cash tumbled out. The ensuing investigation revealed various types of wrongdoing. Kentucky was barred from postseason play and subjected to recruiting restrictions for two years, and the ESE (Eddie Sutton Era)—1986–89—ended.

That Pitino has succeeded as well as he has is a tribute to both his image and his philosophy. He's the very model of the modern, go-getter college basketball coach. He's so dapper that *Gentleman's Quarterly* magazine is featuring him in a coming issue, so entrepreneurial that he already has a Lexington restaurant ("Bravo Pitino") that bears his name.

His philosophy is based on his observation that long-range, three-point field goals are worth one point more than the regular kind. His teams throw up treys at every opportunity and play pressing defense when they don't have the ball. The idea is to leave foes gasping and in arrears.

Pitino has done this at the other stops in his busy career, the previous one being with the NBA's New York Knicks. He's had five different jobs since 1983, but now swears eternal fealty to the blue and white. The only flies in the local ointment, he says, are news folks who speculate that he might not stay here forever.

The Wildcats were 7–2 in the won-lost column before Saturday, and their date with Louisville seemed pivotal. Not only were the visitors unbeaten in six starts, but if you asked UK fans which one game they'd like to win most every year, they'd probably say the one against UL.

The two schools are such hot rivals that from 1922 to 1983, they met only when forced to by the vicissitudes of postseason tournaments. Louisville was hot to trot throughout that period, but UK, traditionally the state's top basketball dog, said no, reasoning it had more to lose than to gain. It was only after UL rose to national basketball prominence under Coach Denny Crum that the state's populace and politicians insisted on yearly meetings.

Crum, too, has had some hard times of late. His teams—NCAA champs in 1980 and '86—often scored in triple digits, but stories last year in the *Louisville Courier-Journal* revealed that many players he'd recruited scored in single digits—of a possible 36—on the ACT college entrance exam, and that just six of the 37 young men who played for

UL in the 1980s got their degrees within five years. The school declared itself behind Crum and recently extended his contract into 1998. But with bonuses based on his players' academic performance.

Kentucky had won six of the nine games since the series was renewed, but the perception of how far the state hoops balance had shifted was reflected in a UK fan's sign at Rupp Arena Saturday. "Move Over Denny, It's Rick's State Now," it read. Time was when no UK fan would concede that Kentucky was ever UL's domain.

UK fans can rest easy for another year, because their boys won on Saturday, 103–89. They did it as they usually do, with three-pointers and the defensive press. They hit on 11 of 21 trey tries and pressed the more athletic but younger Cardinals into 13 giveaways via steals.

John Pelphrey, a skinny senior averaging 13 points a game, scored 16 in the first seven minutes, including 4-for-4 from three-point land, to give UK a 29–19 lead, and UL never got closer than four thereafter. He led Kentucky with 26 points, followed by 25 for sophomore Jamal Mashburn, a muscular New Yorker who'll someday earn his living from the game.

Crum, ever the educator these days, said that teams learn when they make mistakes, and his boys created lots of "learning situations." Said Pelphrey: "Coach likes for us to start thinking about our next opponent right away, but this was a big win. We can enjoy it for a whole day, maybe."

Mark Coomes, *The* (Louisville) *Courier-Journal*

MIRACLE OF MARDI GRAS HAD MANY HEROES

This game is still referenced as a beacon of hope for any basketball team that's being blown out. Kentucky trailed LSU by 31 points with 15 minutes remaining before scratching out a four-point win. This story claims that Duke bested this comeback with a 32-point rally versus Tulane in 1950, but the latest NCAA record book lists the Blue Devil comeback as 31 points, the same as Kentucky's against LSU. The game didn't start until 9:30 PM eastern standard time, so deadlines didn't allow newspapers time to properly recap such a historic event. This Courier-Journal *article was actually printed February 17, 1994, two days after the game was played.*

Louisiana State players, shuffling around in stunned silence, began to take questions. There was only one to ask.

What happened?

"One of the greatest comebacks in college basketball is what happened," said forward Clarence Ceasar, who didn't need a record book to tell him he'd wound up on the wrong end of history.

The University of Kentucky erased a 31-point deficit with 15 minutes to play Tuesday night and beat LSU 99–95. NCAA records said it was the biggest comeback in collegiate history, surpassing Duke's 29-point rally against Tulane in 1959, but further research showed the Blue Devils actually trailed by 32 before winning 74–72.

Missing the record doesn't diminish the feat. The game was, UK coach Rick Pitino said, "the most unbelievable thing I've ever seen."

Some were calling it "The Miracle of Mardi Gras," a serendipitous mix of guts, skill, and luck that senior guard Travis Ford said was even more heavenly than UK's electrifying 104–103 overtime loss to Duke two years ago. (Duke always seems to get that extra point).

The Duke loss is considered by some the greatest game in college hoops history, and the LSU win might be the most preposterous. The Wildcats, who scored only 11 points in the game's first 11 minutes, scored 62 in the final 15:34 to reverse a 68–37 deficit.

There's no one key play in a 35-point turnaround. Such phenomena are powered by bursts of excellence provided by many people, such as:

> Chris Harrison and Rodrick Rhodes, who scored eight and seven points, respectively, in a 24–4 run that slashed LSU's 31-point lead to 11, 72–61, with 9:52 left;

> Jeff Brassow, who twice hit back-to-back three-pointers to single-handedly fend off LSU counteroffensives;

> Walter McCarty, who scored a team-high 23 points, including a clutch three-pointer with 19 seconds left that put UK ahead 96–95—its first lead since 1–0; and

> Ford, who had 10 points and 12 assists, but his biggest contribution was the never-say-die leadership that pulled the rally together.

"When it got to 31, I gathered the team together at midcourt and told them, 'We're going to win this game,'" Ford said. "'We are not leaving this building until we win. I don't care if it takes all night.' We had lost two in a row, and we were not going to lose another."

Pitino ditched his suit coat (which he never does) and immersed himself in the job of erasing a monstrous lead one possession at a time. The coach never panicked, and neither did the team.

Brilliant though it was, UK could not have forged such a rally by itself. Legendary comebacks require some measure of ignominious collapse. The New York Mets needed Bill Buckner and the Wildcats needed LSU.

The Tigers unraveled like a bad alibi down the stretch. They took bad shots (going 6 of 18 from the floor in the final 15:06), bricked free throws (missing 9 of 16—including the front end of three one-and-ones from 10:45 to 2:19), and routinely eschewed the patient execution of their half-court offense.

Their primary ball handlers suffered from brainlock and butterfingers. Ceasar undermined his career-high 32 points and game-high 10 rebounds by committing four of his five turnovers in the second half, while forward Jamie Brandon committed four of his six.

Andre Owens, an otherwise steadying influence who had three assists and no errors after halftime, dribbled straight into a UK trap. To avoid a turnover, he had to squander LSU's second timeout with 12:22 still to play.

"I would've liked to have had the timeout," LSU coach Dale Brown said.

What he'd have accomplished with it is unclear at best. LSU called three timeouts in the second half, and its lead shrunk immediately after each. UK had a 5–2 spurt after timeout number one, a 13–2 run after number two, and a 3–0 spurt after number three, which came with 11.5 seconds left and the Tigers down by one.

LSU's ineffectual play in the final 15 minutes appeared to indicate one of two things: a strategy poorly devised or poorly executed. Either way the onus is on Brown, who's no stranger to strategic meltdowns.

Ask Indiana coach Bob Knight. LSU had the Hoosiers down by 12 late in a 1987 NCAA tournament game. Knight said he wasn't worried: "I looked down the floor and saw Dale Brown, and I knew, well, we had a chance."

Indiana won 77–76.

Tuesday was the kind of against-all-odds, total-team performance of which coaching clichés are made. But you can be certain that every John T. Wooden wannabe from Seattle to St. Petersburg will soon inform his troops of "The Miracle of Mardi Gras."

Jerry Tipton, *Lexington Herald-Leader*

WILDCATS' OT THRILLER A WORK OF HEART

On an annual basis, Jerry Tipton probably contributes more column inches about college basketball than any other writer in the country. The Lexington Herald-Leader *beat writer since the early 1980s, Tipton's full-page Sunday notebook column (a testament to both his tireless approach and his readership's vociferous appetite for all things Cats) is read by coaches and fans across the country. Here he reports on Kentucky's improbable 1995 SEC tournament championship game win over Arkansas, in which Big Blue trailed by nine with 1:39 left in overtime.*

Not all eyes were on Rodrick Rhodes as he tried to win yesterday's game for Kentucky by making either of two free throws with 1.3 seconds left. Freshman Antoine Walker couldn't bear to look at Rhodes at such an emotionally charged moment. So he looked into the Georgia Dome stands as he stood along the lane.

By chance, Walker saw another Chicagoan, Isiah Thomas, as Rhodes began to shoot the first free throw. When the former NBA great made eye contact with Walker, he gestured a message. Thomas patted his breast.

You gotta have heart.

Kentucky showed plenty. Even Rhodes's two misses, though a personal calamity, did not prevent Kentucky from winning. Neither did a 19-point first-half deficit. Unbelievable as it seemed, neither did a nine-point deficit with barely 90 seconds left in overtime.

Despite it all, Kentucky beat Arkansas 95–93 in the Southeastern Conference tournament championship game.

"They were dead three or four times against a great, well-coached basketball team," UK coach Rick Pitino said. "This is the proudest moment of my coaching life."

Reserve point guard Anthony Epps, a hero when it mattered most, confessed that Kentucky's don't-ever-give-up optimism weakened as the game went along.

Arkansas zipped to a 35–16 lead inside the first 11 minutes. Worrisome? "Not really," Epps said. "That was the first half."

Arkansas scored the first seven points in overtime and led by nine with 1:39 left. "You really get tight then," Epps said.

"It didn't look good," teammate Mark Pope said. "Ninety-nine times out of a hundred, we wouldn't win this game."

Arkansas badly beat Kentucky from the three-point line much of the game, but especially early. Six three-pointers propelled the Razorbacks to the 19-point lead. "They were killing us with threes," Pope said.

The Hogs' 11th trey, by Clint McDaniel, seemed most crushing. It capped Arkansas's run of seven straight points to start the overtime.

When Corey Beck drove through the Cats for a layup, the lead stood at 91–82 with 1:39 left.

"I kind of went oh [shoot] myself," UK reserve Chris Harrison said.

Walker, who was voted the tournament's most valuable player, sparked a winning rally that saw Kentucky outscore Arkansas 13–2 in the final 92 seconds. He drove for a layup with 1:32 left. More important, star Corliss Williamson fouled out on the play. Walker's three-point play reduced UK's deficit to 91–85.

"At that point, when he left the ballgame, that kept us from getting the ball to him," Arkansas coach Nolan Richardson said. "That's what we would have done. On that foul, we lost an important ingredient of putting the game out of reach. It made a big difference in the ballgame."

Williamson's team-high 22 points helped repel UK's repeated runs at Arkansas.

Pressure defense helped UK finally break through. "It was a tiring game," Pitino said. "If we were going to shoot gaps and make steals, it was at that point."

Arkansas mishandled an inbounds pass, leading to a Pope tip-in. That made it 91–87 Arkansas with 1:15 left.

When the Razorbacks missed four of six free throws in the final 1:11, that created an opportunity.

Kentucky, which hadn't led since Andre Riddick's two free throws nine seconds into the game, reduced the deficit to 93–92 when Walker posted up for a basket with 25 seconds left. That capped a career-high 23-point game.

Epps gave Kentucky the lead. Arkansas's Mr. Clutch, Scotty Thurman, took an inbounds pass and, when immediately trapped, tried to pass back to Beck. Epps knifed into the passing lane, missed a quick shot, then got fouled trying to put up another.

"It really wasn't me that made the play," Epps said. "It was made by the trap by Antoine and somebody."

Epps's two free throws put Kentucky ahead 94–93 with 19.3 seconds left.

Thurman, the man most responsible for Arkansas's 9–1 record in games decided by five points or less this season, took the decisive shot. Walker's well-positioned defense made it an unlikely three-point rainbow from, oh, 25 feet that hit harmlessly off the front of the rim.

"Coach had told me he likes to drive and push off," Walker said of Thurman's knack for winning games. "I just tried to keep a hand in his face. I couldn't believe he shot it from so far out."

Arkansas, which had won 10 straight, couldn't believe it had lost.

"Kentucky can't play with us," said Beck, the Hogs' emotional leader. "We just hurt ourselves. It was like we were out there walking around at the crucial time. It was crazy."

It was also exciting. Thrilling. Memorable. Satisfying.

"It doesn't get any better than this," Pope said.

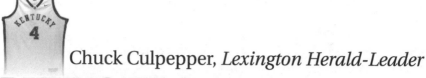

Chuck Culpepper, *Lexington Herald-Leader*

PITINO FINALLY COMPLETES HIS LONG WALK TO AN NCAA CHAMPIONSHIP

Chuck Culpepper's moment-by-moment account of Rick Pitino during Kentucky's 1996 national championship win over Syracuse provides a unique perspective on the Wildcats' sixth title.

And for precisely his 600th game as a head basketball coach, Rick Pitino walked out to the floor last night, alone; his expression, serious; his entry, well after everyone else's; his clothing, exceptional; this, the ritual to which Kentucky has become accustomed these past seven seasons. After those 599 other walks, in sickness and in health, this was the 600th, the one with the big reward looming close to midnight in exchange for all the lonely steps of the previous 599.

He clasped his hands. He looked a shade shy of queasy. For the 600th time. After 435 college games (316–119) and 164 professional games (90–74), this was the largest, the one all the daydreams had contained, the one to stamp him a winner forever, right there in the record books. Kentucky would beat Syracuse for the NCAA championship at Continental Airlines Arena, bringing all the seriousness and the hand-clasping and the near-queasiness to one golden nugget of a conclusion. Six hundred games to get to a huge championship night. Many guys take longer.

He sat down. The players walked out for the tip-off shaking hands and merging fists. He sat down there next to Kentucky equipment manager Bill Keightley, his knees apart, hands together, 600th time. Best time. Tip-off. Antoine Walker missed a shot. Pitino turned and barked something to associate coach Jim O'Brien. Syracuse possessed, couldn't convert. Kentucky went into its offense; the seat beside Keightley got white and vacant.

Just like always.

All Keightley's lonely sits through these things, the results visible in his expression, beaming or fretting, about to become rewarded. Pitino knelt in front of the scorer's table, just like always, knees pointed out, game under way, shouting instructions. "Reverse it! Reverse it!" The soundtrack of Kentucky basketball, fall 1989–spring 1996. Kentucky couldn't score. Pitino left the kneel, stalked back down the bench to the baseline, hands on hips. The procession of Kentucky basketball 1989–96, through the rise from probation to the winning seasons to the 1993 Final Four to the disappointment of Birmingham to this year of high expectations and high elevations.

Syracuse went ahead 2–0 on an offensive-rebound layup by John Wallace. Pitino turned sharply, snapped some words. Mark Pope, the transfer center from Seattle, bounced up, ripped off his warm-up sweater, the urgent insertion, the need to talk one-to-one with somebody out there, the ritual. Antoine Walker came to the bench. Kentucky had the ball. Pitino moved back down, always moving, front of the scorer's table, kneeling, propped up by two fingers, the index and the middle. "Reverse it! Reverse it!"

That considerable larynx, about to get the best off-season break it ever had.

It wasn't a great game. It was just the best game, the 600th. Jason Cipolla of Syracuse hit an open layup, bringing the first ritualistic gritting of teeth. Eight to four, Kentucky. A lead, but always striving for more. About to come, more. Wallace made a three-pointer in front of Walker; Walker came out; Pitino knelt in front of Walker, shouted. There was a foul on Ron Mercer, and the voice came crying out, "That's a ba-a-ad call!" Seat between Keightley and O'Brien, still empty. Another foul on Kentucky; Pitino, as if sprouting out of the baseline, barging down the sideline, in front of the bench, to the scorer's table, flinging his hands in the official's direction. A timeout at 7:59 of the first half, Syracuse ahead 21–20, Pitino, right leg crossed over the left, instructing.

By halftime, after some of those patented Pitino-ball runs, Kentucky held a 42–33 lead, and Pitino filed out, arms flapping, eyes focused on the floor, 600th halftime, best halftime. One half to go to the prize.

Syracuse stayed ornery and drew to within 48–46 by outscoring Kentucky 13–6, and it was time for a 20-second timeout, a proactive Pitino timeout, making his way to the floor, meeting the player (Jeff Sheppard) halfway, smiling a bit at first, then leaning in. All the cajoling of all the years, Boston University, Providence, New York with the Knicks, Kentucky, all about to rise to the nice, noisy pinnacle.

Here a three-point shot by Tony Delk, flying out of the corner, flying down toward the end of all the Pitino 17-hour workdays, the days when there wasn't time for food, the middles of the nights looking at film clip after film clip. It dove down and in. Pitino pointed frantically to the floor. The official didn't need the help: foul, four-point play. Kentucky led 59–46. Eleven minutes to the payoff.

Now it was a matter of holding off the Orangemen and their considerable fight. A tense matter. A timeout at 64–60 and 5:24. An enormous tip-in by Walter McCarty, the player Pitino pursued out of Evansville, to stretch the score from 64–62 to 66–62 when things were getting tight. An enormous three-point shot from the left side by Derek Anderson, the player who came to Pitino when Ohio State busted. An enormous save by McCarty to Pope, the player who came to Kentucky looking for a transfer school and fell in love. A knocked-away Syracuse pass by Pope with 1:06 to go and the lead only 72–67. Pitino, waving his hands, quieting an "SEC" cheer with Delk at the line and 43 seconds to go.

All that work, all those 599 games, and then an insuperable lead of 76–67, with 2.3 seconds left, so Pitino turned around, seat still empty, to O'Brien and assistant Delray Brooks for a cluster hug. Out of that came Pitino, out of his 600th game, to the hugs from his athletics director, his wife, anyone in sight, to the winners' podium, to the place he always hoped all that effort would take him.

William C. Rhoden, *The New York Times*

DUKE-KENTUCKY II: A SEQUEL TO REMEMBER

Ask any Kentucky fan to name the greatest UK-Duke game of all time, and this 1998 contest—not the 1992 Elite Eight loss—wins in a land-slide. The fact that the rest of the nation points to that game in 1992 is still baffling to many folks in Kentucky, especially considering Tubby Smith's first UK team rallied from a 17-point deficit to earn a Final Four berth en route to another national title. The New York Times, *however, instantly recognized the classic nature of the game.*

Sequels are very rarely as good as the original. As Kentucky Coach Tubby Smith said on Friday when he was asked about the classic 1992 Duke-Kentucky game: the stars have to be right.

For long, agonizing stretches last night, the stars were all out of kilter for Kentucky. The explosive Wildcats, whose signature through-out the National Collegiate Athletic Association tournament had been torrid starts, found themselves down by 18 at one point in the first half, and down by 17 in the second.

But Kentucky clawed its way back, and this game lived up to its billing. In fact, this game nearly duplicated the 1992 classic, all the way down to the final dramatic inbound play.

In 1992 Duke trailed by one point with 2.1 seconds left to play. Last night Duke trailed by two points with 4.5 seconds left to play.

In the 1992 game, Grant Hill took the ball out and threw a full-court strike to Christian Laettner, who nailed the winning basket at the buzzer. Last night the Duke freshman Shane Battier, the player with the strongest arm, took the ball out and looked deep. But this time the deep routes were covered. Battier fired a midcourt pass to the fresh-man William Avery. Avery dribbled frantically over the halfcourt line and fired a desperation shot as an entire arena held its breath. Avery's shot slammed off the backboard and into the waiting hands of Kentucky's Scott Padgett, who grabbed it, covered it, and finally flung it away as time expired. It was a fitting end to two classic weeks of college basketball. The tournament now heads to San Antonio and the Final Four.

After yesterday's game, Smith acknowledged the connection to six years ago. "I'm sure our fans and players feel that they have been exonerated," Smith said, half-jokingly. "I think we may have exorcised that 1992 loss to Duke. This was just a great, great college basketball game."

Earlier, someone asked Duke Coach Mike Krzyzewski if, maybe for a split second, he felt a sense of déjà vu as the game wound down to the same play in the final seconds.

Close, he said. But this time there was one crucial difference.

"I would have felt like that had we had a full timeout left," Krzyzewski said. For all the elements that make for great contests—the surges, the comebacks, the attacks and counterattacks—this classic turned on the razor's edge of one crucial decision.

With five minutes and 47 seconds left, Duke found itself clinging to a 72–71 lead. The Blue Devils had watched their 69–52 lead slashed to ribbons by the Wildcats' withering full-court defense and uncanny in-your-face shooting. After a Kentucky miss, Duke nearly lost the ball to pressure, and Roshown McLeod, the Blue Devil senior, used Duke's last timeout.

"I knew we needed the ball," he explained afterward in Duke's quiet locker room. "So my first instinct was to call a timeout. I thought if we could get a basket there, we could gain some momentum."

In the short term it worked. Duke scored four straight points and led 76–73 with 4:21 left to play. But in a classic chess match like this, when long-term strategy ultimately decides the game, McLeod's decision proved fatal. Tubby Smith, his team fresher and sensing the kill, kept the clock moving. Duke led by 77–73, then by 79–75, then Kentucky went on a 10–2 run and led by 85–81 with 16.7 seconds remaining. Smith had four timeouts and saved them like money in the bank. He wouldn't call another timeout until 4.5 seconds were left and Kentucky was leading, 86–84.

"That was a crucial point in the game," Smith said of McLeod's timeout. "I didn't want to call timeout; I wanted to continue the attack and keep on pressing. Mike is too smart a coach. I didn't want to give him time to adjust."

Success and victory balance on such a fragile precipice.

In the opening stretches of the game, Kentucky players seemed to have momentarily forgotten the formula that brought them here: a withering press from beginning to end. After waltzing through the South Regional from blowout to blowout, Kentucky was met by a hurricane of Duke offense as the Blue Devils gave Kentucky a dose of its own explosive medicine. They hit the Wildcats with a furious assault, and before anyone knew what happened, Duke led by 38–20. In the second half, Kentucky trailed by 17 with 11 minutes to play.

"I don't look at the scoreboard," Smith said when someone asked about the thoughts running through his mind at this point. "I don't look at the score. I just knew we had to make something happen. I knew they were getting all the loose balls and all the long rebounds. I wanted to stop play and change the direction of the way things were going."

And so he did. And so they did. After Duke's final timeout, Kentucky outscored Duke by 15–10 and Smith, in his first season as head coach, takes Kentucky to the Final Four for the third straight season.

Last year the Wildcats were runners-up; in 1996 they were national champions. As Smith spoke, his proud father, Guffrie Smith, 80, and his mother, Parthenia, 76, sat in wheelchairs in back of the interview area, savoring this moment. Tubby was the sixth of 17 children.

"He's always been a good fellow," his father said. His mother smiled. "Never had any problems," he said. "He's a great man."

Today, thousands of fans in Lexington will say "Amen" to that.

Pat Forde, *The* (Louisville) *Courier-Journal*

VICTORY A TRIBUTE TO COACH AND TEAM

Pat Forde has moved from UK beat writer to Louisville Courier-Journal *columnist to national acclaim on ESPN.com, all the while providing talented insights into the world of Wildcats basketball. Here he looks at Kentucky's remarkable 78–69 win over Utah in the 1998 national championship game.*

Remember the Alamodome, University of Kentucky fans.

Remember this game.

Remember this moment.

Remember this season, this team, this coach.

You will see other basketball national championships won at the current rate of collection, you might see another one 12 months from now. But remember with special fondness what these Comeback Cats did and how they did it.

The No Star Team conquered the Lone Star State. Kentucky conquered Utah 78–69 with a simple yet mysterious and all-too-often-elusive gift: thirteen guys. Together as few groups are.

At a program that has created a modern-day dynasty, these altogether-unlikely heirs to the throne will be cherished. At a program where special teams are legion and come with their own nicknames, this charismatic collection of spare parts has defied naming and defied belief. At a program where special wins are a dime a dozen, this team's final three victories will stand among the most glittering gems in the jewelry case.

Down 17 to Duke last week, the Cats came back.

Down 10 to Stanford on Saturday, the Cats came back.

Down 12 to Utah last night, the Cats came back.

They were led back by Orlando "Tubby" Smith, the son of a sharecropper, one of 17 children and, oh yes, an African American. For that reason, this seventh UK championship resonates in a deep and different way from the other six.

If 1978 was important because it finally moved UK past the Rupp Era, if 1996 was important because it gave closure to the rehabilitation of a pariah program, then 1998 is important because it gives final closure to UK's bitter racial legacy.

Not even 30 years ago, someone of Smith's skin color had never put on a Kentucky uniform, much less been put in charge of the Kentucky program.

Now that a black man has hung a banner at UK, we can all move on. We can simply call Smith a championship coach.

Here's to the man who stepped into a thankless task and turned it into a chorus of "Thank yous!" Here's to a patient man coaching in his first year at what is a historically impatient place.

Here's to a man who never panicked, who resisted any urging or counseling to remodel his team, instead tinkering here and there to make it better. While the rest of Cat Nation occasionally shrieked its concern, Smith simply stayed the course.

And when the calendar turned to the postseason, UK was ready. Do not doubt Smith's March mojo. With this victory, he's 12–4 as an NCAA tournament coach. That .750 winning percentage is second among active coaches, trailing only Duke's Mike Krzyzewski (43–12, .782).

Last night was Tubby at near perfection. Foul trouble plagued his centers, but Smith never wavered from his season-long habit of subbing players out with two fouls in the first half and three early in the second half. He didn't flinch at sending shaky lineups onto the court, even when they looked way too small or you wondered where the points would come from. He benched both his backcourt stars, Final Four Most Outstanding Player Jeff Sheppard and Wayne Turner, for long periods, and it paid off.

He called just a single timeout in the game's first 39 minutes, and it turned the game around. Down 64–60, Smith gathered his veteran team and sent it out to simply rip the game away from a Utah team that had dominated much of the night.

Utah was taller. Utah was thicker. Utah was, in some key positions, better.

But Utah was not tougher. Nobody in America is. Kentucky outscored Utah 18–5 in the final five and a half minutes to become champions.

As has been the case all year, contributions came from an unlikely amalgam of players.

Sheppard again made big baskets this time off the dribble, not from beyond the three-point arc.

Wayne Turner rose up after an ugly first half with some key plays in the final minutes.

Forward Scott Padgett helped keep UK close in the first half and played huge interior defense down the stretch against the monstrous Utes.

Nazr Mohammed was offensively big early. Jamaal Magloire was big at both ends in reserve.

Cameron Mills, of course, made two amazing three-pointers.

Allen Edwards lowered his head and attacked the basket, drawing defenders so he could dish out five assists.

And Heshimu Evans, the kid they call "Mu," was the guy who turned the game around with a slew of heroic plays at both ends. Remember the AlaMu, UK fans.

Combine it all and somehow, all of a sudden, these are the champions.

If you say you believed this was possible on December 27, when Louisville shocked the Wildcats on their home court, you were either nuts or lying.

If you say you believed this was possible on February 1, when Florida came into Rupp Arena and dominated Kentucky, you were either nuts or you were lying.

If you say you believed this was possible on Valentine's Day, when Mississippi strolled into Lexington, Kentucky, and won there for the first time since 1927, you were either nuts or you were lying.

But the patient man and his indomitable players never doubted. At least not openly. Same as when they were down 17 to Duke— nobody dared say die.

When coaches want to show future players videotape of how to play as a team, this UK group would be a good one to start with.

Looking at this modest UK team next to its heroic accomplishments is like looking at the ancient Egyptians next to their pyramids. *How did they do it?*

But it is no longer time to puzzle over how this happened, but to simply appreciate the fact that it did happen. It is done. Kentucky is champion.

Remember the Alamodome, UK fans. And the team that won it all here.

Dan Wetzel, CBS Sportsline.com

IT'S KENTUCKY—NOT FLORIDA—THAT LOOKS LIKE NUMBER ONE ON THIS NIGHT

Only two opponents ranked number one by the AP have played Kentucky in Rupp Arena. Both left with losses. Florida arrived in downtown Lexington as the freshly minted top team in the nation but left with a humiliating 70–55 loss as the Wildcats' suffocating defense throttled the Gators. National college basketball columnist Dan Wetzel captured the February 2003 mania for CBS Sportsline.com. The visitors from Gainesville weren't the only ones to come unglued by the withering UK attack, as this Kentucky team became the first SEC squad in 51 years to sweep both the league regular-season schedule and tournament without a loss.

Florida arrived here in the Big Blue Nation on Tuesday sporting the nation's number one ranking, a 14-game win streak, and a whole lot of firepower and swagger.

They left more whipped than a guy at a Dixie Chicks concert.

Kentucky turned the nation's top-ranked team and serious challenger to its SEC throne into a holiday tournament patsy in one of the most impressive and overwhelming performances of the season, dropping the Gators 70–55 in a game that wasn't even close to that close.

"Kentucky just outplayed us in every facet of the game," said Gators coach Billy Donovan.

That about sums it up.

This was a complete show of force for the Kentucky program—from the ridiculous defensive intensity, to the asylum-crazed crowd, to the way it thoroughly gutted the Gators to post its 11th consecutive victory and look like a true threat to capture another national championship.

At least as long as they play defense like this.

"We are just getting so much confidence," said center Jules Camara. "We know if we play defense like this, nobody can beat us."

A comment like that could be chalked up to the afterglow of a huge victory, but Camara is absolutely correct. Donovan became the seventh coach in a row who wondered after the game if his team is really this bad offensively or if the Wildcats might just be that good.

"I've learned to stay away from making rash and crazy comments after games like this," he said.

Good move. You could say Florida stunk offensively Tuesday, and with just six first-half baskets, six assists for the game, and 34 percent shooting, you have evidence to support the claim. But this is what Kentucky does.

This incredible Cats run started at halftime of the January 14 game at Vanderbilt. UK was screwing around that night, trailing Vandy by eight when coach Tubby Smith challenged his guys to have some pride. The rest is history.

Kentucky (17–3, 7–0) hasn't lost since. It hasn't been close. Only one team, number 10 Notre Dame, got into the 70s.

In the past seven games, opponents (four of whom were ranked) are averaging 57.3 points. Five of the past six have shot less than 40 percent.

Sure, the Gators were more confused than a butterfly ballot. But that seems to be a recurring theme.

Maybe Kentucky lost too many games (three) early in the season to be ranked number one, but right now no one is playing any better. The Wildcats aren't just beating teams, they are taking their manhood and leaving the entire program questioning every facet of its existence.

What does Donovan say to his team as they watch the tape Wednesday, other than "put it out of your mind?" Florida tried to execute and hustle; the Gators just didn't stand a chance.

Kentucky's defense does more than just lock you up, it so completely frustrates you, so thoroughly knocks you out of your game plan that chucking up 20-footers and leaving your coach with his head in his hands actually seems like a good idea. Sure beats trying to feed the post.

"I think we played into Kentucky's hands with too many guys playing one-on-one," said Donovan.

Might we repeat, this was the number one team in the nation.

Give Donovan credit—he coached his team until the final buzzer, not so much because he thought Florida could storm back and win this one, but so maybe, just maybe, they wouldn't go into the game in Gainesville on March 8 totally afraid.

That kind of admirable effort and determination is why Donovan was able to get Florida to the top of the national polls for the first time in school history. They got it to 15 only because Donovan left his starters in when Smith sent in his reserves.

So Florida (18–3, 7–1) played hard to the end. But that didn't mean the end wasn't hard.

This game was over in the first half, when the Cats turned up the defense and Cat fans turned up the volume until Rupp was in bedlam. In the final 12-plus minutes of the first half, Florida managed a single basket and Kentucky enjoyed a series of alley-oops, dunks, and fast breaks that put the arena-record crowd of 24,459 into a state of euphoria.

"Our crowd and our players were very into it," Smith said. "I could feel the energy in the building."

Cats fans rightfully pride themselves on not storming the court after victories. When you are the winningest program of all time, nothing merits a clichéd postgame celebration. Not even humiliating number one. So they didn't.

But who knew they would have to restrain themselves from doing it at the half?

In the deep, rich annals of Kentucky basketball, all 100 seasons of it, there aren't too many halves that were better played and more satisfying to watch than the first 20 minutes against Florida.

It was a total annihilation, a browbeating, an early round knockout that unfortunately for the Gators had to continue.

This is the kind of night Kentucky fans live for. An SEC contender showing up with press clippings and a puffed-out chest and then everyone whooping it up as Cliff Hawkins dominates the perimeter, Gerald Fitch drains three-pointers, Marquis Estill swats shots with menace, and Keith Bogans plays like a champion.

You could say Kentucky fans are a bit cocky when it comes to SEC supremacy. And you'd be correct. But 41 titles will do that to you. Just as an 11-game win streak and a style of play that wins championships will get the Big Blue Nation dreaming of an April in New Orleans.

Was this a statement victory, someone asked Hawkins?

"The only statement we want to make is in April," he said.

Nice answer, but wrong. This was a statement. This was Kentucky showing the nation and the SEC that it is very much for real and the loss to Louisville five weeks ago is a distant, distant memory. This was the Wildcats once again humbling a traditional football school that has eyes on its SEC supremacy.

"I hope the best is yet to come," said Smith.

Georgia, you've been warned.

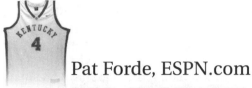

Pat Forde, ESPN.com

GUARD POWERS CATS TO WIN OVER ARCHRIVAL

Patrick Sparks's storybook game against Louisville in December 2004 was the stuff of Hollywood, topped off by three game-winning free throws with 0.6 seconds remaining. ESPN was one of the many national media outlets to tell the tale of this Kentucky hero.

In a state where every boy grows up with visions of game-winning shots dancing in his head, Patrick Sparks lived the Ultimate Kentucky Fantasy on Saturday afternoon.

The scrawny, pasty, burrheaded point guard had a game against archrival Louisville that will be talked about in this hoops-obsessed state until Sparks is gumming his food in a retirement home.

They'll talk about how the kid who embodies the myth and lore of Kentucky basketball sank three free throws with 0.6 seconds left to beat the Cardinals 60–58 in perhaps the most thrilling of the 36 series meetings.

They'll talk about how the kid who grew up in Central City, an old coal-mining town of about 5,500 in the western part of the state, wouldn't let the Cats lose, scoring 12 straight points in the second half to lead a stirring comeback from 16 points down.

They'll talk about how the kid who spent hours shooting day-dream game-winners in the backyard, at the school gym—"anywhere you have a hoop," according to his stepmom, Michelle—busted a game-high 25 points on the hated Cards.

They'll talk about how the coach's son stabbed Kentucky hero-turned-villain Rick Pitino in the heart with cat-burglar calm and Ken Jennings wits under incredible last-minute pressure.

They call this annual bloodbath The Dream Game. For Patrick Sparks, it was the Wildest Dreams Come True Game.

"It's the old kid-in-the-backyard, game-on-the-line kind of thing," said Sparks's dad, Steve, who had to watch the game on television from London, Kentucky, two and a half hours away, where his Muhlenberg

North High School team was playing in a tournament. "It's a classic. You hear kids talk about it all the time."

Now they'll be imitating Sparks, who just earned himself a first-class spot in the Kentucky basketball annals. Elected office and endless free meals are now in his future.

"It's a big moment," Sparks allowed, with customary stoicism.

It's a moment that reverberated from Paducah in the western tip of the state to Pikeville in the Appalachian Mountains. Ending Pitino's two-year reign of terror over his former school means that much to Kentucky fans—and the fact that the hero was a homegrown boy originally passed over by the Wildcats makes it all the sweeter.

"When you think about how it turned out," Sparks said, "it's just crazy."

It's truly crazy that Sparks now owns arguably the biggest made free throws in Kentucky basketball in 25 years, since Kyle Macy dried his hands on his socks and made the free throws that beat Magic Johnson and Michigan State in the 1978 regional finals. Lacking a scholarship offer from the Cats after a stellar career playing for his dad at Muhlenberg North, Sparks went to Western Kentucky. When coach Dennis Felton left that school for Georgia after Sparks's sophomore year, he took it as his opportunity to try a bigger stage.

The first place he visited—Louisville. Pitino offered a scholarship and thought Sparks was set to commit—but when he returned home from his campus visit there was a message waiting from Tubby Smith. When Sparks told Pitino that he wanted to visit Kentucky before making a decision, Pitino saw the writing on the wall and rescinded his offer.

Smith got it right on the second try, getting the guy he passed over in favor of Josh Carrier and Brandon Stockton. Sparks came into this game as UK's second-leading scorer and top assist man—and now, after Saturday, as its undisputed king of clutch.

For a long stretch of the second half, Sparks was the only thing keeping Kentucky in the game. Louisville had dominated the first half, getting easy basket after easy basket and throttling the Cats' half-court offense for a 32–16 halftime lead. It was UK's fewest points in a half since a 3-for-33 shooting disaster against Georgetown in the 1984 Final Four.

Kentucky came out with increased energy in the second half, but Louisville still maintained a 10-point lead with seven and a half minutes to play. That's when Sparks went crazy, hitting three straight three-pointers and then converting an old-fashioned three-point play to make it 54–50 with 2:55 to play.

A thin and tired Louisville team, which was hurt badly by an eye injury that took out freshman center Juan Palacios for the final 17 minutes of the game, tried to hold on. In the final 87 seconds the lead changed hands five times, with the deciding sequence going down like this:

Louisville led 58–57 when Sparks drove to the basket. Cut off on the baseline and in trouble, the junior quickly called timeout with 4.8 seconds left. Even then, Sparks's brain was in high gear; he knew that a baseline out-of-bounds situation usually yielded a good scoring opportunity.

Time left—4.8 seconds. It would last an eternity for Pitino and the red majority of the 20,088 fans in Freedom Hall.

Smith drew up a new play in the huddle. He sent 7'3" Shagari Alleyne down the lane as a decoy and then had wingman Kelenna Azubuike fan to the sideline for the pass.

At that point, Louisville's defense broke down. Larry O'Bannon stayed with Azubuike, but Francisco Garcia—who performed well below All-American level—left the inbounds man to double Azubuike on the sideline. The inbounds man was Sparks.

Azubuike took two dribbles away from the double-team—but also away from the basket. For an instant it looked like he would have to fling up a no-hope shot, but Azubuike jumped and dumped a pass back to wide-open Sparks in the corner.

Sparks set his feet behind the three-point line and saw Ellis Myles rushing to close out. In a remarkable display of last-second cool, Sparks pump-faked, sending Myles flying toward him. Then Sparks jumped—not straight up but a foot to his right, initiating contact with Myles and selling it to the officials by crashing to the floor.

Foul. Three shots. Freedom Hall went crazy.

But Sparks still had to make the free throws.

While the officials huddled around a monitor to determine how much time should be put on the clock, Sparks paced around the foul line. His teammates didn't come near him.

"It was kind of like when a pitcher has a no-hitter going," Sparks said. "Nobody wants to be around him."

Smith called him over. Sparks didn't want to go. Finally he did.

"Where you going for Christmas?" Smith asked, trying to break the ice.

"Going home," Sparks responded and then went back to the foul line.

"I was just ready to knock 'em down and get out of here," said Sparks, an 85 percent foul shooter.

"I was confident," said Michelle Sparks. "I haven't seen Patrick miss many free throws, and I've seen him shoot a lot."

Swish. Swish. Swish. Ballgame.

Kentucky led for less than six of the game's 40 minutes—but it led at the end. Along the way it matched its largest comeback from a half-time deficit in school history.

In a hotel room in London, Kentucky, Steve Sparks and his Muhlenberg North players were bouncing off the walls.

"I was worried about the people in the room below," Steve Sparks said. "I hope they weren't Louisville fans."

During the game, Steve stayed in constant phone contact with Michelle, seeking the details he couldn't get on TV. His instructions to his wife before the game: "Look, you can't go crazy on me. I've gotta get some info."

Michelle maintained her poise during the game—although she might have been the only one in an emotionally overwrought Freedom Hall. Back home in Central City, Steve is sure they were all going nuts.

Until yesterday Central City was most famous as the hometown of the Everly Brothers. Now it's also the hometown of a certifiable Big Blue hero, whose performance Saturday will be talked about until Patrick Sparks is an old man.

"It's one of those wonderful stories, to be honest," Steve Sparks said. "It's truly a Cinderella story."

Jeff Sheppard, MVP of the national championship game, dunks for two points in Kentucky's win over Utah for the 1998 NCAA title.

Section II
THE TEAMS

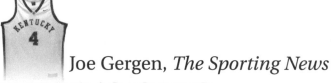

Joe Gergen, *The Sporting News*

RUPP'S CATS FIDDLE AWAY

The Sporting News's Joe Gergen has recapped every basketball national champion, and here he takes a look at Rupp's fourth title squad, the 1958 Wildcats.

Adolph Rupp not only coached them, he named them.

The players who represented Kentucky in the 1958 season were far from the Baron's finest, but collectively, they ranked among his favorite teams. Their achievement exceeded all expectations.

The coach had little reason to believe this group would be the one to restore Kentucky to the throne of college basketball, to earn the Wildcats another championship that he felt had been unfairly denied the school.

These players weren't particularly big or talented, they had contributed to a disappointing finish the previous year, and then they opened the '58 season by losing three of their first seven games.

"We've got fiddlers, that's all," Rupp decided. "They're pretty good fiddlers. Be all right entertaining at a barn dance.

"But I tell you, you need a violinist to play in Carnegie Hall. We don't have any violinists."

Thus was born the legend of the "Fiddlin' Five."

It was a team without a dominant player, a major star. Not only would no Kentucky player win consensus All-American recognition after the season, but the Wildcats didn't even place a man on the All-Southeastern Conference first team.

Kentucky compensated for its shortcomings with balance, its ability to run Rupp's intricate offensive patterns with precision and an uncanny knack for winning tight games.

Even in claiming the conference title and an automatic berth in the NCAA tournament, however, the Wildcats did not appear a formidable contender for the national championship. Their overall pre-tournament record of 19–6 was subpar for a team coached by Rupp.

Working in Kentucky's favor was a schedule that granted the Wildcats a home-state advantage throughout the NCAA meet. In fact, the Mideast Regional was being staged at the Memorial Coliseum on Kentucky's Lexington campus for the second consecutive year. And Freedom Hall in Louisville would host the Final Four in 1958.

The Wildcats, featuring four seniors and a junior, were at their best in the regional, blowing past Miami of Ohio, 94–70, and Notre Dame, 89–56. And while they were having their way, many top teams suffered stunning upsets.

West Virginia, number one in both wire-service polls, was a first-round loser to Manhattan in the East Regional. Cincinnati, ranked second, was beaten by Kansas State in the Midwest Semifinals, and San Francisco, rated third in one poll and fourth in the other, was toppled by Seattle in a Far West Semifinal.

Suddenly, a path to the top had been cleared.

And Rupp wanted nothing so much as he did a fourth championship. He still was steaming over NCAA sanctions that forced Kentucky to cancel its 1953 season.

The Wildcats, playing with a vengeance the next season, won all 25 games but declined to participate in the NCAA tournament because their three best players were graduate students and ineligible for post-season competition. The 1954 national tournament was won by a La Salle team Kentucky had beaten by 13 points during the season.

All of this preyed on Rupp's mind. Again and again he had vowed, "I will not retire until Kentucky wins another NCAA championship."

Now, surprisingly, he had the opportunity. At 56, Rupp was taking his fiddlers down the road to Louisville for the big dance.

The other three national semifinalists were Temple, Kansas State, and Seattle. Of the Final Four teams, Temple was the quickest, Kansas State the tallest, and Seattle the possessor of the most extraordinary player, Elgin Baylor.

If Kentucky had any edge, it was in teamwork.

Although the Wildcats had handed East Regional winner Temple one of its two regular-season defeats, the Kentucky triumph in December was anything but decisive. It required, among other things, three overtimes and a half-court shot by Vern Hatton. And that game had been played on Kentucky's home floor.

Once again Kentucky and Temple were matched up, and once again they played an enthralling game. Sparked by Guy Rodgers, the brilliant guard, Temple held a 60–59 lead with 23 seconds left.

During a timeout, Rupp told the Wildcats to place the ball in Hatton's hands. The 6'3" senior guard promptly drove the lane, ducked underneath traffic around the basket, and dropped in a layup. Temple had time to reverse matters, but sophomore Bill "Pickles" Kennedy couldn't connect with a Rodgers pass and Kentucky hung on to win, 61–60.

With 6'8" Bob Boozer, 6'9" Jack Parr, and 6'8" Wally Frank on the front line, Kansas State was the most imposing team in Louisville. Parr had been particularly effective in the regular season against Wilt Chamberlain, helping coach Tex Winter's team supplant Kansas as the Big 8 Conference champion. But Kansas State's trio was no match for the smooth and powerful Baylor, who led Seattle to a 73–51 romp in the other semifinal.

Baylor had been unstoppable during the season. He averaged more than 30 points per game in the Chieftains' freelance attack. The 6'6" youngster from Washington, D.C., who had taken a football scholarship at the College of Idaho and transferred to Seattle after proving himself in basketball, had a bewildering series of fakes and, in apparent defiance of gravity, was able to hang in the air long after defenders returned to earth.

There was considerable doubt in Rupp's mind that Kentucky could contain Baylor. His strategy was to attack Baylor at the defensive end and force him into foul trouble. To that end, he was aided by John Castellani, the young Seattle coach.

Rupp had expected Baylor to draw the defensive assignment on 6'7" center Ed Beck, who didn't look to score but was content to rebound and play defense. For that reason, Rupp and assistant Harry Lancaster had planned to have Beck drive to the basket around set screens. But Castellani chose to send Baylor, who was playing with injured ribs, against John Crigler, a quick 6'3" forward. During an early timeout, Crigler was instructed to drive the baseline whenever possible.

As a result, while Baylor hurt the Wildcats on offense, the Seattle star had his hands full with Crigler on defense. The Chieftains raced to a 29–18 lead, but Baylor was charged with three fouls in the first 10 minutes.

Determined to keep him in the game, Castellani switched to a zone defense, with Baylor on the back line, and slowed the tempo on offense. The outside shooting of Hatton and forward Johnny Cox brought Kentucky back, cutting the deficit to 39–36 at halftime.

"Baylor had those three fouls," Castellani said, "and with his rib injury, we had to slow it down to protect him. My object was to go to the locker room with a lead and only three fouls on Baylor."

The strategy succeeded in that regard. And Seattle pushed the lead to 44–38 in the first three and a half minutes of the second half. It was then that Baylor drew his fourth foul, curtailing his natural aggressiveness for the rest of the game.

Kentucky seized the [opportunity].

Cox, a 6'4" junior, led the charge. Exploiting the Chieftains' zone, he scored 16 of his 24 points in the final 15 minutes. It was his long jump shot that tied the score at 56–56. The Wildcats finally grabbed the lead at 61–60 on a hook shot by reserve Don Mills, who entered the game when Beck got into foul difficulty attempting to handle Baylor.

Cox followed Mills's basket with another jump shot and Kentucky, thanks to an 8–0 run, was en route to victory and the unlikeliest of its four championships.

The gallant 25-point effort by Baylor was not sufficient against Kentucky's superior team play. Seattle's consensus All-American was accorded outstanding player honors, but Hatton led all scorers in the title game with 30 points as Kentucky wound up an 84–72 winner. Rupp preened after the trophy presentation.

"These were just a bunch of ugly ducklings," he said. "Not one of them made the all-conference team. And I didn't get a single vote for Coach of the Year, so I know it wasn't overcoaching.

"Frankly, I didn't think we'd get this far."

The fiddlers got as far as any team in Rupp's tenure, and they presented him with what would be his final national championship. For that reason, or perhaps because they squeezed so much out of their abilities, they remained special to him until the day he died in 1977.

"This team played the best, as a unit, of any of the championship teams I've coached," he said that night in Louisville, "each player making up for the particular weaknesses that the others had."

The 1958 Wildcats made such beautiful music together that no one missed the violinist.

Billy Reed, *Lexington Herald*

CHEERS, TEARS, AND BIG CROWDS AS "RUPP'S RUNTS" COME BACK HOME

Much has been made of Texas Western's win over the Wildcats in the 1966 national championship game, but few people outside of Kentucky understand the love affair UK fans had with Rupp's Runts. Billy Reed gives a firsthand account of the team's return to Lexington the day after the season had ended.

"Rupp's Runts," easily the most popular team ever to play basketball for the University of Kentucky, came home yesterday.

Their many, many fans in Fayette County didn't forget, either, despite a 72–65 loss to Texas Western Saturday night in the championship game of the NCAA tournament.

About 800 greeted the Wildcats' chartered airplane at Blue Grass Field, ignoring a request by airport officials to wait for the team at Memorial Coliseum.

Mrs. Donald Summers, 346 Hill 'n' Dale Road, waved signs saying, "Welcome Home, Our Champs" and "You Will Always Be Number One to Us."

Everyone else either applauded or yelled as the Wildcats, led by Coach Adolph Rupp, came off the plane and on to a red carpet.

Among the last off was senior Larry Conley, who looked tired and worn after playing two tournament games with a bad case of the flu.

Meeting Conley and wrapping his arm around him was Bob Wright, who coached Conley at Ashland High and now coaches at Morehead State University.

The players looked miserably sad as they lined up behind a microphone. Rupp stepped forward to speak as the crowd pressed closer.

"Wonderful Winter"

"Thank you for coming out," began Rupp in his world-famous Kansas twang, "but I'm afraid that we're not number one today."

The crowd protested vehemently.

"To be honest, and that's the way we always want to be, we didn't play well. It's a shame we didn't play as well as we're capable.

"But these boys have provided us a wonderful winter of entertainment. Only one team in the nation has a better record, and that team beat us last night.

"This is a wonderful basketball team."

Rupp then introduced seniors Conley, Tommy Kron, and Larry Lentz. He was interrupted by a couple of jets thundering low over the airport.

"That's a salute to the number one team in America," airport manager Logan Gray said. The crowd cheered again and Rupp resumed introductions.

"We want to thank all of you for coming out," he concluded. "Maybe if you stick around another year, we might do a little better."

Parade Next

The jets thundered overhead again, drowning out applause as the players climbed into open convertibles provided by the Committee of 101.

Rupp climbed into a white police car that led the parade and thanked Gray for the reception. The cars snaked from the airport escorted by motorcycle police.

People lined the route from the airport to the Coliseum. There were young girls in slacks, old ladies with tears in their eyes, little boys in sweatshirts all waving and shouting in tribute to the little team that did big things.

Rupp, for the most part, watched the scene in silence. He waved occasionally or made a comment. Once, he blew his nose.

"I don't believe a team in the nation has ever been as popular as this crowd," he said, waving at a little girl. "They got more publicity than any team ever got."

He wore a brown suit that has been his trademark in marking up the most fantastic coaching record in the history of basketball.

"Conley played as well as he could," he said, "and the others didn't. We've got to be factual about it. Even he didn't play an outstanding game, but then he wasn't physically able."

He looked out over the rolling hills of Central Kentucky, passing swiftly now as the motorcycles sped up and turned on sirens.

"It's remarkable how it's greened up just in the three days since we've been gone," he said. "I guess it's been warm."

The motorcade went down High Street, turned right on Rose Street, then right again to Memorial Coliseum, where more cheering people waited in front.

Welcome at Coliseum

Rupp hopped out, shook hands with UK president, Dr. John W. Oswald, and waited for his players to assemble. Some were besieged by autograph hounds before they could even get out of their cars.

"Autographs, later, fellows," Rupp said paternally. "Let's get inside now."

The crowd made way and the players filed inside. Kron, bringing up the rear, stopped to shake a few hands.

Rupp led the team through a curtain and on to the Coliseum floor, where a crowd of more than 5,000 stood and gave them a five-minute ovation as they sat in chairs in the middle of the floor.

Once they stood in acknowledgement.

When the noise subsided and the fans were seated, UK athletics director Bernie Shively stepped to a microphone.

"Very seldom do you see such warmth, enthusiasm, and affection when a team loses," he said. "I think this is a tribute to the young men on this team and we thank you very much."

Oswald called the Wildcats "the greatest ambassadors from our university and Commonwealth as any aggregation we've ever had."

He praised a semifinal victory over second-ranked Duke, called the loss to Texas Western "one of the greatest efforts any group of Kentuckians ever put out," and asked a young fan to hold up a sign.

It read: "In our book, you will always be No. 1," and the fans cheered some more.

Praises Fans

Rupp received a standing ovation from players and fans.

"There aren't any better fans in the world than those in Central Kentucky," he said. "I have a suitcase full of telegrams. I didn't realize how many fan clubs we have."

Among those sending telegrams were the Centerville Fans Club ("Why, that's where my farm is") and every state college in the state.

"We received a goodly number of honors this year," Rupp said. "I was named Coach of the Year, but here are the boys and other coaches who made me Coach of the Year.

"I didn't get Coach of the Year last year."

He told the fans that Kentucky wasn't up for the Texas Western game and couldn't get its shots to drop.

Introduced next were assistants Harry Lancaster and Joe Hall, and trainer Spike Kearns. Rupp then asked Conley to say a few words.

Seniors Speak

The blond senior from Ashland flushed and stood with hands jammed in pockets and head bowed while the fans roared their welcome.

"You-all might as well stop that," he said, "because you're just making it harder for me… I was real sorry we couldn't bring back the big one."

Tears came to his eyes and a sob welled up in his throat.

"Well," he blurted out, "we went out there and tried."

He turned around and walked off as the fans cheered some more.

"I've never seen a finer example of courage," Rupp said.

Kron was next to the microphone. More under control than Conley, he thanked the fans for turning out at the airport and Coliseum.

"We played a bad game, probably our worst of the season," he said "It came at an unfortunate time. We played 27 good ones and two bad ones.

"But I want to thank you for the wonderful enthusiasm, and I want to challenge Pat, Louie, and Thad, and all the rest coming back. You know where your goals should be set and strive for them in the immediate and distant future.

"Thank you from the bottom of my heart."

Above and Beyond

Rupp introduced the rest of the team while the fans cheered and then delivered his concluding remarks.

"There's a little sticker down below on that trophy that says second place," he said. "We'll have to take that little sticker off."

Everybody laughed.

"After last year, to have a comeback like this is remarkable and a credit to the boys.

"When you consider that 500 teams start out and they tell us finally that we couldn't have the fifth one (NCAA title), that's cutting it pretty thin.

"We have some good boys back and we'll try to do better next year. Thank you."

Fans stampeded the floor and mobbed Rupp and his players with autograph requests.

"If my husband would see me, he'd just die," laughed a middle-aged woman emerging from a crowd around Conley.

Police finally moved in and saved Rupp, Conley, and others from suffocation. The fans applauded as they left.

A wrinkled old lady had been standing off watching the autograph mess.

"I think that's above and beyond the call of duty," she snapped.

Yes, ma'am. But that's the kind of season it was.

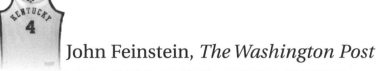

John Feinstein, *The Washington Post*

BOOK ON KENTUCKY: ONLY TITLE PAGE IS FLAWED

The much-ballyhooed 1983–84 Wildcats lived up to their hype—SEC regular-season and tournament champions, NCAA Final Four berth, and a number three final ranking. Featuring the Twin Towers of Sam Bowie and Melvin Turprin, Joe B. Hall's squad drew the attention of The Washington Post's *John Feinstein, who wrote this overview during the nonconference portion of the schedule.*

Six years have passed since the last national championship at Kentucky. No titles, only memories.

The memories are bad ones. A 1980 loss in the regionals on the hallowed hardwood of Rupp Arena. Then, humiliating early round NCAA losses to Alabama-Birmingham and Middle Tennessee. Finally, the loss in the regional final to Louisville last season. A great game, a great team, but Louisville? The poor relations who just aren't mentioned in polite company?

Coach Joe B. Hall fought long and hard against the concept of Kentucky blue sullying itself by mingling with Louisville red during the regular season. But this year, it came about anyway.

Fans here *know* that nobody beats the Wildcats. The Wildcats may beat themselves, may get beat by the referees, but they don't get beat by a superior opponent. Can't happen.

The players live in Wildcat Lodge, digs so splendid that several years ago the NCAA ordered Kentucky to make the rooms smaller and allow other students to live there, too. Those who live among the players are chosen by Hall and his staff. They are good students. "Examples to our players," says one Kentucky official. Read more closely: most are tutors.

"You can't understand what it's like to be a basketball player at Kentucky," says Sam Bowie, a 7'1" senior who is the most revered of the revered 12. "You're treated by the people like an immortal, a god. You are a role model for people. Sometimes, I wish I could be just another 22-year-old. But more often than not, I don't wish that."

This season, the number two Wildcats have Bowie back after he missed two seasons because of a fractured shin bone. They have 6'11" Melvin Turpin, recruited as insurance for Bowie four years ago, but now probably the best offensive center in the country.

They have Jim Master, a deadeye shooting guard. They have Kenny Walker, the 6'8" sophomore who may have been the country's best freshman a year ago. They have three point guards who do different things at different speeds. They have Winston Bennett, a freshman who has already fought Bowie in practice and probably will fight him again before season's end. They have talent, depth, and experience.

"When I think about what this team can be, I get excited," said Hall, who seemingly gets excited about once a decade. "We can be a mighty good team. Mighty good."

It has been six years.

The Recovering Star

For two years, Sam Bowie answered the same question 10 million times. Would he come back? When he first hurt his leg in 1981, he was expected to be out six weeks. He missed two seasons.

Bowie thought he would be in the NBA now. In 1979 he was rated only slightly behind Ralph Sampson among high school seniors. Kentucky's signing of him was supposed to guarantee at least one national title, maybe two. Four years have produced two years of early elimination and two years of watching.

Now Bowie is back for a fifth year. He is healthy. He will graduate this week with a degree in communications and take graduate courses next semester to stay eligible.

In the two years Bowie sat, Turpin became a star. Now he plays center and Bowie plays forward.

"Before I got hurt I was used to shooting the ball at least 15 times a game," Bowie said. "Now, that isn't going to happen. Our offense just isn't designed that way. It's designed for the center. If I get double figures in shots in a game, that will be unusual. I'm not bitter about that. I know I can contribute without scoring all the points.

"But people expect me to score 20 points a game because that's what I did before I got hurt. Now it's different. Our offense is a good one and there's no need to change it as long as we're going well.

"Two years ago, when I first was out, I used to pull Melvin off to the side to try to teach him some things. Now, I'm learning things from him."

Bowie insists he is almost 100 percent. He says he could score more if asked to. The coaches say he may be 50 or 60 percent, but nowhere near 100 percent. "I don't think a player who has been out two years can be 100 percent in one season," said Hall. "Sam's going to keep coming, keep getting better. But he's been away a long time."

Bowie struggled before the season. He only took 14 shots the first three games and his once-smooth jump shot has looked awkward. Last weekend, though, he went to the boards aggressively during Kentucky's Christmas Tournament, getting 15 points and 14 rebounds in the final against Brigham Young.

Bowie, slender with short, curly hair, reads the newspapers. He has read about all he has accomplished just by coming back and playing. "I haven't accomplished anything yet," he said. "I always knew I would come back, I never questioned it. For two years, I always thought it would be next week.

"People ask me if I can be the old Sam again. The old Sam didn't win any national championships. I don't want to be him again. I want to be a player that wins a national championship.

"When I do that, I will have accomplished something."

The Coach

In his first 11 years as Kentucky's coach, Joe B. (for Beasman) Hall had a record of 250–82, an average of almost 23 victories a year. He has been to the Final Four twice and won the national championship in 1978. He won the NIT in 1976.

In return, he has been allowed to keep his job.

To Kentucky fans, winning isn't a privilege, it's a birthright. Hall is not a man who inspires great warmth, so he must win to keep the masses happy.

"There are always pressures which go with opportunity," Hall says.

The opportunity, every year, is for Hall's team to win the national championship. Kentucky gets great players—so many that it is the most whispered-about program in the country. Leonard Hamilton, the associate coach who does most of the recruiting, talks often about "witch-hunts," the never-ending search for the so-called real story of Kentucky basketball.

Hall looks professorial with his wire-rimmed glasses and conservative suits. He has a Kentucky gentleman's southern accent that turns Wyoming into Wahoamin' and makes words just a little bit longer. He rarely smiles in public and has a reputation for being humorless.

"Coach Hall's just like anyone else," Bowie said. "I've gone fishing with him and if he slips on a rock, I laugh because I know if I slip, he's going to laugh at me."

His reputation is that of a screamer, a coach who demands much of his players. This year, people have noticed a change.

"I don't know why he isn't getting on us in practice as much as he used to," Turpin said. "But I sure like it better this way."

There appear to be two reasons for Hall's change. One is the makeup of this team. There are two fifth-year players and three fourth-year players. "Anytime you have a senior ball club, it's a little more relaxed for the coach," Hall said. "If they haven't picked up what you're trying to tell them after three years, it's give-up time."

The seniors on the 1978 team—Rick Robey, Mike Phillips, Jack Givens, James Lee—gave the impression their championship season was an endless grind, one they could not wait to see end. "If we win the national championship, it will have been worth it," Robey said the day before the national title game.

This team appears to be much looser. What's more, there are two new assistant coaches, Jim Hatfield and Lake Kelly. Both have been head coaches. Hall listens to them.

Hall seems to have grown used to the pressures that go with his job. "At Kentucky, if you started five freshmen, people would expect you to contend for the national championship," he said. "It goes with the territory."

The Key

Bowie attracts the national press. But Dicky Beal may ultimately decide the fate of this team.

Beal is a 5'11" senior who has never been a starter at Kentucky. He played behind Dirk Minnifield for three years, and last January, in a game against Auburn, he hurt his knee. He had arthroscopic surgery twice and still the knee hurt. He consulted another doctor in Cincinnati and in August went to Georgia for a third arthroscope.

Beal, still delicate, hardly played in Kentucky's first two games. The word was he was through, that he could run straight ahead but not laterally. But against Kansas 14 days ago, Beal played 19 minutes. Then last Saturday against Brigham Young, Beal put on a nine-minute display of breathtaking basketball.

Kentucky was already on a roll, in the process of a 41–8 streak, when Beal went to work. In nine minutes he scored eight points and had six assists. Having not played at full speed for almost a year, Beal was so exhausted that Hall had to call time to take him out.

"It felt good to play like that again, it had been so long," Beal said. "I figure my job when I'm in there is to push the ball, try to make things happen, get us on a roll and keep us on a roll."

Without Beal, Kentucky uses sophomore Roger Harden and freshman James Blackmon as point guards. Harden is a role player, a smart, walk-it-up player who will run the offense efficiently and make the open shot. Blackmon is a raw talent who likely will be a star. But neither has Beal's experience or quickness, even after knee surgery.

"Dicky is a special player," said Master. "You don't have to wonder if he'll get you the ball, if he'll make the pass. You just know he will."

Beal almost went to De Paul four years ago, changing his mind at the last moment. He has had mixed feelings about that decision since then because he has done a lot more watching than playing. Last Saturday, though, after his nine-minute masterpiece, he was almost glowing.

"Probably awful cold in Chicago right now," he said with a wink. "Feels nice and warm here."

Practice

It was cold in Rupp Arena when the players started drifting out to warm up.

A half-dozen reporters were waiting at courtside. Kentucky does not allow the press into its plush locker room, but it does allow pre-practice interviews. But even as the players talked, managers prowled around glaring at the interlopers and reminding the players they should be warming up.

This was not a long or tough practice. But it was apparent that Hall has turned much of the teaching over to the new assistants, Hatfield and Kelly. Hatfield was coach of Mississippi State and Hardin-Simmons and Kelly was coach of Austin Peay.

So when Kentucky worked on its press offense, Hatfield did most of the talking, Hall occasionally jumping in with a comment or to point something out to an individual. When it was time to work on defense, Kelly took over.

"The assistants pretty much run things in practice every day," Master said. "Coach Hall has confidence in them and so do we."

Hall got angry once, when his experienced starters passed the ball to the wrong man against the press. "*Think out there!*" he yelled, his voice booming through the building.

The rest of the practice was sedate, the Wildcats going through their paces for a weekend they knew would not provide them with terribly tough tests. Bowie, with two finals to take, appeared far more concerned with them than with Wyoming or Brigham Young.

As the team dispersed, Master kept yelling, "Number four, number four, tomorrow we get [win] number four." No one paid much attention.

Game Night

The consolation game of the University of Kentucky Invitational had been going on for about 30 minutes, and about 3,000 people were moving restlessly around Rupp Arena. Most of the fans were still across the walkway in the Hyatt Hotel, waiting for the Wildcats to take the court 90 minutes later.

Bluegrass music reverberated off the hotel lobby's walls, and the privileged patricians with UK tickets sipped their drinks in preparation for the evening's romp.

Most of the men wore suits, the women expensive dresses. Kentucky basketball is to Lexington what an embassy party is to Washington. There is little yelling or pregame cheering. The Wildcats have a game to win and the fans have a game to watch, simple as that.

For 20 minutes, though, there is a problem. His name is Devin Durrant. The 6'7" Brigham Young senior scores 22 points during the first half of the championship game, and at halftime the Cougars lead, 36–34. There is concern from most of the 24,098 people.

Grim-faced, the Wildcats retreat to their locker room. There, Hall gives them a tongue-lashing. "What I said to them," he said later, "can't be repeated."

The players, however, do not find Hall's words surprising. "We knew we played lousy," Master said. "We were just as angry as he was."

"People stereotype people," said Bowie. "I'm sure everyone was probably running around here saying, 'Boy, Joe's probably giving it to them good in there.' But he didn't yell that much. He didn't have to."

Whatever was said, the Kentucky players came out of the locker room silently except for Beal, who ran from one teammate to another shouting, "Let's get it going now."

They did. From 40–40, they blew Brigham Young back to Utah with a 41–8 burst. Turpin got the ball down low and was unstoppable. Bowie hit the boards hard. Master made a couple of jumpers. And Beal was unreal. By the time the devastation was over, the final was 93–59 and even the usually placid Kentucky fans had screamed themselves silly.

"I don't know anyone in the country who could have stopped them when they got going the way they did," said Durrant, who finished with 33 points. "They just have so much, so much."

The Kentucky players shrugged off the compliments. They know they are good. They are 6–0 now, but that is a long way from the Final Four in Seattle. Master said simply, "I hope we're better than this. After all, Brigham Young isn't exactly the most talented team we'll face this year."

Hall was so happy with the second half, he actually seemed relaxed when the game was over. "After a while I just breathed a sigh of relief and became more cheerleader than coach," he said. Then he smiled. Briefly.

It is only December. Six victories cannot wipe out six years of bad memories.

Pat Forde, *The* (Louisville) *Courier-Journal*

SENIORS TOOK THE DESPAIR OUT OF CLIMB FROM OBLIVION

Like the 1966 Rupp's Runts, the 1992 Wildcats—dubbed the Unforgettables—warmed the hearts of all Kentuckians despite ending their season with a bitter loss. Pat Forde, at this time the UK beat writer for the Louisville Courier-Journal, *followed up his game story with this look back at this remarkable team.*

Save your newspaper clippings, videotapes, and mental images of this basketball team, University of Kentucky fans. You may never see another one like it.

You won't see a four-man senior class, three of them homegrown, so popular.

You won't see a group turn darkness into light, depression into glee, bad rep into good rep, so deftly.

"The guys who stayed just wanted to get the program going back to where it was," fifth-year senior John Pelphrey said. "I think we did that, and we enjoyed it. It's just hard to believe it's over."

It ended with stunning suddenness Saturday night in Philadelphia, when Duke foreclosed on the dream by beating the Wildcats 104–103 in an all-time classic.

It ended a season that began breathtakingly high—a number four ranking—then appeared headed straight for the scrap heap after all of two games.

An 18-point pounding at the hands of Pittsburgh in the Preseason NIT commenced statewide worrying.

But you *knew* they'd bounce back. Big. Victories over Indiana, Louisville, and Notre Dame saw to that. Things proceeded at a lovely pace until...

It was time for more statewide worrying, as the Cats were thumped three out of four. Tennessee, then Arkansas, then Louisiana State hammered UK. The question became: would this team be ready when it got its four-years-in-the-waiting shot at the NCAA tournament?

Once again, the Cats regrouped. They won 11 of their last 12 regular-season games, capping it off with a tear-drenched good-bye to Pelphrey, Richie Farmer, Deron Feldhaus, Sean Woods, and legendary Cawood Ledford on Senior Day against Tennessee.

It was on to the Promised Land, the postseason, for the first time since 1989. Kentucky must have been living right in the interim, because it got all the breaks it needed—including a meeting with Louisiana State without Shaquille O'Neal—to get to the final game of the Southeastern Conference tournament. Once there, no more breaks were needed as UK unleashed all the pent-up frustration of probation in an 80–54 pounding of Alabama.

Suddenly that number four preseason ranking didn't look as crazy as coach Rick Pitino made it out to be—and the big prize lay ahead.

The NCAA tournament. A shot at it all. A long shot, to be sure, but a shot nonetheless.

It ended up not being that long a shot after all. In fact, the shot Woods took that appeared to beat Duke and put UK in the Final Four was only about eight feet. The only thing was: the defending national champions had destiny, Christian Laettner, and two seconds on their side.

Laettner's 17-foot jumper ended the game and the dream. But after the emotional wreckage has been repaired, this 29–7 team can take its place as one of the most beloved in UK history.

To some it will be *the* most beloved. Included in that group is Pitino, who said on a couple of occasions this season that no senior class could beat this one out for the top spot in his heart.

It was Pitino who perhaps captured the spirit of this whole thing Saturday morning in Philadelphia. Out for his normal jog of a few miles, the coach got so pumped up he wound up going nine.

He topped it off by running up the steps of the Philadelphia Art Museum—the same steps another famous overachiever once ran up in *Rocky.*

Remember, Rocky lost in the end, too. But he went the distance, and afterward the champ knew he'd been through a war.

Now, what about a sequel?

Kentucky has the heavyweight to build around in sophomore Jamal Mashburn, who lifted his game to new heights in the postseason. If O'Neal, Harold Miner, and Jimmy Jackson—all juniors—make themselves eligible for the National Basketball Association draft, Mashburn just might find himself billed as the best player in the country next year.

To look at it through Big Blue–tinted glasses, here's what his supporting cast will feature:

- An improving Gimel Martinez at center;
- A healthy Travis Ford, who will undergo off-season knee surgery, at point guard;
- A more consistent Dale Brown—the ultimate X factor this year, you never knew when he'd be awesome or awful—at off-guard;
- Somebody at small forward. Could be Jeff Brassow, if he recovers from reconstructive knee surgery. Could be prize recruit Rodrick Rhodes, if he becomes academically eligible. Could be junior-college forward Cleveland Jackson, whom the Cats have been taking a look at.

Even under the best of circumstances, that lineup is not terribly imposing. But as long as Pitino is stomping his high-priced loafers on the sideline, you'd give his team a chance for more surprises.

Could it do what this team did? Perhaps. Anything's possible in basketball. But the intangibles the 1991–92 Kentucky Wildcats had—the chemistry, the love of he program, the guts—may never be seen in such quantities again.

"It's been a great ride," Pelphrey said. "We've had a lot of fun, enjoyed it, and we'll miss it."

They'll be missed in equal measure.

I AM KENTUCKY, AND
I LOVE SURPRISES

Tubby Smith's first UK team—the Comeback Cats—rallied from double-digit deficits in its last three games en route to the school's seventh national title. It was the third straight Wildcats team to play for the national title. The Lexington Herald-Leader's *Chuck Culpepper penned this recap for the newspaper's special publication commemorating the school's eighth national title.*

A foreign visitor arrived at the gate of Kentucky basketball in the early spring of 1998. Kentucky, hospitable in general, let in the visitor.

Kentucky was curious about the visitor, warmed up to the visitor, and learned to relish the visitor.

The visitor was called surprise.

Even across a century rather storied, Kentucky had never been acquainted with such pleasant surprise. It had become a basketball kingdom where championships were expected (if still celebrated) every now and then and pre-championship defeats were met with dismay, with coping, and eventually with hoping again. If there was a national championship on Kentucky's horizon—and there had been six prior to 1998—generally it was because Kentucky had spent a few years constructing it. Courting the talent. Welcoming the talent. Meshing the talent. Overwhelming opponents with the talent.

Yet as day after night after day rolled by in early April 1998, there seemed to be a lingering inconceivability about Kentucky's seventh national title. Could that really have happened?

Which, of course, was part of its appeal.

So was the fact that it was playing under the program's first black coach, in his first season at Kentucky—Orlando "Tubby" Smith, who, when the magic was complete, got a ride out of the Alamodome in San Antonio on the shoulders of his players.

So was the fact Kentucky's coach and its players and its camaraderie proved irresistible, winning over many Americans who previously could not bring themselves to pull for Kentucky.

So was Kentucky's identity as a starless team in an age of superstardom, attitude, and ESPN highlights seen as achievements. Not one player averaged more than 13 points per game, the team's lowest leading scoring average in 50 years. In the final three games of a thrilling NCAA tournament, Kentucky produced no fewer than eight players you reasonably could peg as heroes.

I am Kentucky, and I gave up on 1998.

I gave up a little bit in May 1997, when Coach Rick Pitino left for the Boston Celtics. That ended eight festive seasons for which any fan should be grateful, and I went hurtling into the frontier of change, an uncomfortable place for hoopaholics.

I gave up a little bit one week later when the university introduced Smith as coach. I knew he had won at Tulsa and Georgia, which is downright hard to do, but I did not know whether he could handle winning in a commonwealth where winning was a birthright. I figured at best it would take him a few years to adjust.

I gave up a little bit in November 1997 when, in the Maui Invitational semifinals in Hawaii, Arizona made the Kentucky basketball team look not only defeated but frightened. Arizona's players said Kentucky's team was not as good as its predecessor, which Arizona had edged in the 1997 national title game. I knew Kentucky would be good, but it didn't seem it would be elite.

I gave up more than a little bit in late December 1997 when Kentucky took a puzzling home loss to a Louisville team that would lose 20 games. Over that, I temporarily lost my marbles, which I am prone to do.

Long strings of wins did not quite sate me, for I am too used to those.

I gave up a little bit the first day of February 1998, when Florida, coached by former Kentucky assistant Billy Donovan and former Kentucky player John Pelphrey, came to Rupp Arena and beat Kentucky's team methodically. Following that, Kentucky eked past Louisiana State at Baton Rouge only by weathering a spate of last-second shots.

I gave up a little bit on Valentine's Day, no less, when Mississippi came to Rupp Arena and beat Kentucky in Lexington for the first time since 1927. I gave up even though the team was 22–4 at the time. Even more than for those outcomes, I gave up because the team appeared muddled, messy, plodding, and unsure of its roles.

Then I certainly gave up a little bit on March 22, when Kentucky trailed Duke 71–54 with nine minutes, 30 seconds to play in the South Regional finals of the NCAA tournament.

And I gave up a little bit on March 28, when Kentucky trailed a bruising Stanford by 10 in the second half of the national semifinal at the Alamodome.

And I gave up a little bit on the night of March 30 when Kentucky trailed Utah, which had cleared out Arizona and North Carolina, by 12 early in the second half of the national championship game.

I am Kentucky; now imagine my unexpected joy.

Imagine how my joy sprouted when Kentucky followed losing to Mississippi by winning at Florida, at home against Georgia, at Auburn, and rather easily at strong South Carolina, looking considerably more fluid in the process and finishing the regular season 26–4.

Imagine how my joy began to gather when the Wildcats tore through the Southeastern Conference tournament at Atlanta looking all of a sudden finely tuned, as tuned as any team in the nation, tuned as well as even the four teams which had spent the season popularly identified as first-rate: North Carolina, Duke, Arizona, and Kansas.

Imagine how my measure of joy annexed some hope to go along with it when Kentucky tore through its first three games of the NCAA tournament, two in Atlanta and one in St. Petersburg, Florida. When it led a perfectly decent Saint Louis team 40–13 in the first half, the score alone conjured memories of the dominant runs to the Final Four in 1993 and the national championship in 1996. When it treated UCLA (which, remember, I don't particularly like) as if it were UC Santa Barbara or UC Irvine, coursing through it 94–68, you might say I was full of hope.

That was two days before March 22.

On March 22, my joy elevated to full roar.

The roar came from all around the court at Tropicana Field.

It was born as tepid applause, when supposedly sub-elite Kentucky, the number two seed in the South Regional, trailed absolutely elite Duke, the number one seed, by 17. That applause acknowledged a three-point shot from the left wing by Heshimu Evans. The score was 71–57.

The applause climbed a notch as of a three-point shot from the left side by Scott Padgett. The score was 71–60. It built still more as of a conventional three-point play by Wayne Turner, driving past Duke's Steve Wojciechowski for a layup and a subsequent foul shot. The score was 71–63. As Kentucky's defense set about doing what defenses do— win championships—the applause mushroomed toward maximal as of an Allen Edwards three-point shot from the right of the top of the key. The score was 71–66. A ball game was on, and it would roll on uninterrupted through the frantic final minutes because Smith, aware Duke had no timeouts left, wisely let it do so.

With one of the more painful defeats of the Kentucky century lodged somewhere in the mindset, Kentucky and Duke went back and forth, tug of war. With Duke's 104–103 victory in a 1992 regional final and Christian Laettner's famous winning shot responsible for a Kentucky wound still open almost six years later, Kentucky trailed

79–77 and missed a shot. A little more than two minutes remained. The rebound came off.

Evans, on the baseline, noticed that every jersey around the perimeter looked blue.

He reached up, batted out the ball.

Cameron Mills from Lexington, Kentucky, caught it and shot.

As the ball sang through the net, my roar reached fruition. This was Kentucky's first lead in the long struggle back. Nothing feeds a roar like a comeback.

But Duke regained the lead, then Kentucky forged an 81–81 tie, and then Kentucky regained possession, setting up unforgettable moment number two. Turner had the ball on the perimeter. He dribbled around a screen. Padgett, who had set the screen, pivoted free. Turner flipped it to Padgett. Padgett let fly.

When this three-point shot too sang through, my roar went past fruition into ripeness. That old wound was about to meet its final healing. Soon Duke was flinging up a hopeless, last-second shot, Kentucky's 86–84 win was in the books, Smith was pogo-ing on the court with his players, and Mills was sobbing into the floor. Soon Duke coach Mike Krzyzewski was stopping several Kentucky players in a hallway to laud them and was saying of them, "They have amazing camaraderie."

Maybe that 32–13 comeback over the last nine and a half minutes helped my spirits a bit the next week in San Antonio, but Stanford's 10-point lead still seemed steep until Nazr Mohammed and Jeff Sheppard formed the rescue. Mohammed hit shots early in the second half. Sheppard went around screens to hit three indispensable three-pointers in the late part of regulation and the overtime. Jamaal Magloire blocked a late shot by the excellent Arthur Lee. Edwards made a long inbounds pass that Turner plucked away from Lee to safety. The 86–85 win was long and rugged.

Still, maybe the camaraderie of the Comeback Cats wasn't enough to overcome Utah, which had routed Arizona 76–51 and outlasted North Carolina 65–59 to show up as a formidable opponent. Through a first half and part of a second, Utah had a clamp on Sheppard and a domination on the boards. Imagine my joy, then, when Kentucky assembled one last comeback, the longest comeback ever in an NCAA title game, with two three-point shots from Evans, two three-point shots from Mills, and a little big baseline shot from Sheppard. A telling microcosm: In Kentucky's comeback from a 64–60 deficit with less than six minutes left to a 70–65 lead, five different players scored.

When Turner dunked with 13 seconds left and the eventual 78–69 victory was secure, the equanimous Coach Smith, sixth child out of 17 born to Southern Maryland farmers, stood at the sideline and pumped his fists slightly.

Imagine my joy as the dark-blue quadrant of the Alamodome stood roaring with a fresh title. Smith kissed Mills on the head. The team stood in a clot and looked upward at the scoreboard video screen, watching highlights of a storybook tournament for which it was a fitting champion. The players carried off Smith, the 46-year-old who had coached the tournament calmly and shrewdly and beautifully and expertly and so singularly maybe nobody else could have done it. Smith kept saying he couldn't believe it. "Did we really just win the national championship?" He kept thanking everybody he had ever met. Outside the locker room, Smith and three players boarded a golf cart to carry them across the dome to the formal-interview room. Smith kissed Evans on his bald head. Sheppard, in the passenger seat of the cart, hugged the driver. That's right. Late in the star-studded, attitude-heavy 1990s, the most valuable player of the Final Four had just hugged the driver. Seems they had formed a quick friendship two days prior. Who couldn't like this team?

I am Kentucky, and I wasn't used to pleasant surprise, but in March 1998 I started to think it was welcome any time.

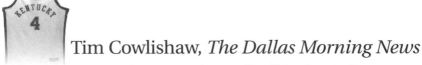

Tim Cowlishaw, *The Dallas Morning News*

KENTUCKY PROVIDES SHINING EXAMPLE

Although they fell short of the Final Four by losing in double-overtime to Michigan State, the 2005 Kentucky team, led by senior workhorse Chuck Hayes, epitomized the selfless approach Tubby Smith demands. The Dallas Morning News's Tim Cowlishaw described this selflessness the morning of the Austin Regional championship game.

No team has ever won in college basketball quite like Kentucky. And in today's game, the Wildcats are winning like nobody else.

The number two–seeded Wildcats are one victory over Michigan State away from a 14th trip to the Final Four. You can argue the case for UCLA having won more titles, but the Bruins did almost all of their winning in one era under one man.

No team has been to as many tournaments or played in as many tournament games or won as many tournament games as Kentucky.

That's what Tubby Smith tells incoming freshmen. "All we promise them is an education and the opportunity to be part of the winningest college basketball program in America," Smith said Saturday.

In his eighth year at Kentucky, Smith is selling something few other elite coaches dare to even try. He's selling selflessness.

Lots of coaches talk a good game when it comes to commitment to team play. But the modern college game is in a star-driven era where the best players stay a year or two on campus before signing up for the NBA draft lottery

Kentucky played 13 players against Utah on Friday night…in the first half. They did that a week ago against Cincinnati, too.

The Wildcats do not have a player who averages 30 minutes per game. They do not have a player who averages 15 points or eight rebounds.

The school with the most basketball-obsessed following in the nation has no stars—not on a national scale, anyway.

But the Wildcats are 28–5, one game from a trip to St. Louis where their one-for-all, all-for-one attitude would be a welcome break from the all-for-me attitude so many other schools bring to the Final Four.

Past Kentucky champions have been driven by star power. Tony Delk, Antoine Walker, Ron Mercer, and Jamal Mashburn led Rick Pitino's winning teams.

But when Smith took over and won a national title in 1998, there was a new game in town. That team didn't have anyone averaging 15 points a game, either.

The player who epitomizes Kentucky's refreshing spirit is forward Chuck Hayes. At 6'6", he is frequently called upon to guard power forwards several inches taller. He has missed one practice in his four-year Kentucky career.

He ranks among the school's top 10 in rebounds, blocks, and steals, and he's in the top 20 in assists. His numbers would be even more impressive if he played more than 30 minutes a game, as he did as a junior.

But this season, no one gets 30 minutes. And, apparently, no one complains about it, either. Certainly not Hayes, the team leader on and off the floor.

"He is not a taker, he's a giver," Smith said. "He is a contender, not a pretender. I call him a servant."

That's what the entire team has become. Smith brought in maybe the best freshman recruiting class in the country last fall. Those players, particularly starters Rajon Rondo and Randolph Morris, have been given their chance to share the spotlight, but they don't command it.

Kentucky has nine players averaging 11 or more minutes a game, with a 10th playing just under 10. That depth allows the Wildcats to do many things.

They can weather foul trouble better than anyone left in the tournament. Against Utah's 7' All-American center, Andrew Bogut, the 6'10" Morris got into instant foul trouble.

For most teams, having their starting center limited to five minutes would have meant an exit from the tournament. For Kentucky, it meant 35 minutes for 7' Lukasz Obrzut and 7'3" Shagari Alleyne.

While they defended Bogut one-on-one, the rest of the Wildcats played the passing lanes so well that Bogut went 40 minutes without an assist as Kentucky won, 62–52.

Against Michigan State, the Wildcats say they will be looking at something close to a mirror image. They face a team that has great athleticism and plays relentless defense, especially on the guards.

"We will have to play a better game against Michigan State to win," Smith said.

If they do, people will see a familiar team in the Final Four. But it's a team with a most unfamiliar method to its basketball madness.

Kyle Macy, who helped lead the Wildcats to the 1978 national title as a sophomore, waves to fans during the 1980 season.

Section III
THE PLAYERS

Tommy Fitzgerald, *The Sporting News*

BEARD THINKS, EATS, LIVES BASKETBALL

A key component in Adolph Rupp's Fabulous Five, Ralph Beard is one of the quickest and most competitive players to ever wear Kentucky blue. This article appeared in a December 1948 issue of The All-Sports News *(which later became* The Sporting News*).*

He was disgusted with himself. He felt disgraced. In his despondency, he was tempted for the only time in his life with a desire to take a drink.

He didn't want to go home. He couldn't face his mother. He was ashamed of himself. Thinking and grieving and crying, he rode around all night in an automobile with an old high school chum.

At 5:00 in the morning, his mother heard a timid knock on the door. She opened it and into her arms, weeping, fell her son, Ralph Beard, one of basketball's all-time great players and still only a senior at University of Kentucky.

"Mom," he sobbed, "I wish I was dead."

What had he done?

Stolen? Robbed? Murdered?

No. He simply had failed to make a single point in a basketball game. That's how seriously this amazing 21-year-old, twice All-American with another season to go, and voted the best player in the nation for two years, takes his basketball. It is this gravity that he has put into his playing that has made this colorful little 5'10", 175-pound guard from Louisville, Kentucky, truly great.

Along with his earnestness go pride and sensitiveness. It was his pride that had been wounded that night in his freshman year of basketball with U of K when he went scoreless at the Jefferson County Armory as Kentucky was losing to Notre Dame. Never before or since has he failed to score in a game. He wanted so desperately to look good that night, too. It was his first appearance before his Louisville home folks since he had left Louisville Male High to continue his athletic exploits at U of K.

"I Wish I Was Dead"

The pressure was on him and he tried too hard. He played a bad game. Nobody knew that better than he did. He felt like a fool.

"Mom," he said, "I wish I was dead."

Mrs. Sue Beard, the mom to whom he is devoted and who has been his chief counselor and inspiration through his remarkable basketball career, consoled him as best she knew how.

Even though she sold him on the idea that life was still worth living, despite a zero behind your name in a basketball box score, Ralph was still down in the dumps while riding back to Lexington, Kentucky, with the U of K team the next day.

He felt, in his warped imagination, that everybody, especially Adolph Rupp, Kentucky's celebrated coach, was ignoring him. Finally Rupp called him back to his seat and gave him a fatherly talk.

"Let's forget the past and think about the future," was Rupp's kind and parting injunction to his young protégé, then only 18.

And think about the future, his and U of K's future in basketball, was all this most serious-minded young man has done from that day. What a steel determination, a burning concentration on one goal can accomplish, Beard has shown. The following season against Notre Dame in the Armory he scored 19 points and tied the great Kevin O'Shea in knots as U of K won, 60–30.

He has a sharp eye for the basket, but his greatest assets as a player are his tremendous speed and limitless stamina. He never lets up once in a ball game. Seldom has he met a guard who can keep up with the killing pace he sets. He simply runs his opponents to exhaustion. Defensively, he has no equal. He hawks his man into helplessness and surrender.

He has made the sacrifices necessary to achieve this endurance and retain this speed. He has never smoked or taken a drink in his life. He has a girlfriend, Ginger Bowman of Vine Grove, Kentucky, but all through last basketball season he didn't date once. He hits the hay regularly at 10:30. He permits nothing to distract him from basketball or to interfere with the rest he needs to play his kind of game.

Basketball is an absorption with him. He has no hobbies, unless it's keeping his scrapbook up to date. He gets so much publicity and so many rave notices he's kept pretty busy pasting them in the book. His studies also take a lot of his time, because he's a serious and conscientious student. He usually gets A's and B's, but occasionally drops to a C during the basketball season, when he has a hard time thinking of anything else but basketball.

Beard is a boy spurred with a determination to become the best at anything he undertakes. He's so deadly serious that he's easily hurt.

Resentment over a remark by U of K's football coach during his freshman year impelled him to quit school.

High School Grid Star

Beard was a star blocking back in high school and continued that sport at U of K, although he went there on a basketball scholarship. Between halves of a game during his freshman year, the only one he played in football, the coach accused the squad of not "having any guts."

Beard got up and began taking off his uniform.

"Nobody," Beard stormed at the coach, "can say that to me and get away with it. I quit."

Teammates influenced him to play the second half because they needed him. Taken out a few minutes before the game ended, he went directly from the field to the dressing room, took off his uniform, and left the University of Kentucky. He was hurt, disgusted, homesick, and disillusioned by the failure of the team to keep in condition.

The next day, he was registered at the University of Louisville. One of his coaches in high school, Pap Glenn, convinced him he was making a mistake. He returned to U of K the following day.

"Ralph thinks that's the most important and the best decision he ever made in his life," Mrs. Beard said.

If he had entered U of L the nation might never have heard of Ralph Beard as a basketball player. He may never have been All-American.

Beard is not a native of Louisville. He was born at Hardinsburg, Kentucky, December 2, 1927. He was a sophomore in high school when he joined his mother, who had moved to Louisville. His parents had become estranged. His father, who had played basketball, football, and baseball for Kentucky Military Institute, now lives in Dallas, Texas.

Ralph was an all-state basketball player at Male High and was acclaimed by many observers as the greatest high school player Louisville had ever produced. His team won the state championship in his senior year, 1944–45.

He was a natural. He wasn't exactly nursed on a round bottle, but he had played basketball since he was three years old.

"His first basket," his mother recalls, "was his nursery chair. He was three then. We had bought him a round rubber ball and his father taught him to pitch it at the nursery chair. Later we got him a real basketball goal and put it on his high chair. Next, when he got a little older, we put the basket above the kitchen door. You could hear the sound of breaking dishes in our house every day.

"When he was about six, we made a regular court in a vacant room we had upstairs. Older boys would come in and play with him. Falling plaster was a daily occurrence. Next we moved the basket outdoors on the garage. The dishes and plaster were safe then."

Until last summer, when he went to London as a member of the U.S. Olympic team, Ralph worked as an instructor during vacation time at a boys' day camp on the grounds of K.M.I. at Lyndon, Kentucky. This gave him daily access to an outdoor basketball court.

Longed to Play in Garden

Ralph's two ambitions, when he left Male High, were to play basketball with U of K and play in Madison Square Garden. He had offers from many schools, including an appointment to West Point, but he figured the surest way to get to the Garden was to play with U of K, annually a power in basketball. He also desired to go to U of K because he admired Rupp's coaching.

His greatest basketball thrill came in the Garden in March, 1946, when he shot a free throw in the closing seconds to beat Rhode Island, 46–45, for the National Invitational title.

Ralph has a brother named Monie, short for Moorman, his mother's maiden name, who hopes to follow in his brother's footsteps. Ralph and Monie don't look alike. Monie is larger, being 6' and weighing 165. When he was in high school, Ralph was a mere 5'9" and 154.

Monie has lettered in four sports—football, baseball, basketball, and track—and is captain this season, his senior year, of the Male basketball team.

Ralph's ambitions when he gets out of Kentucky are to play both professional basketball and baseball, if he can work them both in. He's quite an infielder and has attracted offers from pro scouts. He has displayed his most skill at third base. When his professional playing days are over, he doesn't know whether he'll go into coaching or business.

Like all great athletes, Ralph has tremendous nervous energy. He talks so fast and excitably he almost stutters. He constantly chews gum and is a five-sticks-at-one-time guy. A Lexington druggist provides him with chewing gum free. Last summer at the Olympics, when it was written that Ralph could get no chewing gum in London, an American company sent him a dozen cartons with its compliments.

He says he chews the gum because it keeps his mouth from getting dry.

His play during the last three seasons, however, has been enough to keep Rupp's mouth from getting dry. During those three seasons, Kentucky has won 99 games and has dropped only seven to collegiate opponents. All three seasons the Wildcats ran away with the Southeastern title, captured the National Invitation one year, were runners-up the next, and last year won the NCAA crown and the college championship of the nation.

Ralph's admirers think that if he were in a position to do it over, Dr. Naismith, the inventor, probably would name his sport Basketbeard instead of Basketball.

Billy Reed, *The* (Louisville) *Courier-Journal*

EVEN RUPP SAYS ISSEL MAY BE UK'S BEST BIG MAN SINCE SPIVEY

As this article attests, much was expected of Dan Issel before he even played a varsity game for Kentucky. He, of course, did not disappoint, becoming the school's all-time leading scorer with 2,138 points in three seasons. Billy Reed teased UK fans with this Issel preview during his freshman season of 1966–67.

If you heard someone describe Dan Issel, you wouldn't think he was much different from any other 18-year-old boy.

His favorite recording group is "The Lovin' Spoonful," which is the rage these days among the mop-headed set.

He enjoys a big steak ("you can't beat it") and his favorite author is George Orwell, who wrote *Animal Farm* and *1984*.

And he likes to shoot pool and "mess around" with his roommate, Randy Poole.

So Dan Issel doesn't seem much different, but he is.

You can see that when he puts on a pair of sneakers and starts shooting a basketball in the University of Kentucky's Memorial Coliseum.

"Sensational," Says Baron

At 6'8" and 223 pounds, Issel may be Kentucky's best "big man" since 7' Bill Spivey was stuffing baskets almost two decades ago.

Of course, he's only a freshman, but even such wait-and-see people as UK coach Adolph Rupp and his assistant, Harry Lancaster, are forced to superlatives when asked about Issel.

"We think he's sensational," Rupp said. "We think he's the best center prospect we've had here in some time. He's a big, strong boy and he moves well."

Lancaster admitted that the former all-sports star from Batavia, Illinois, "might very well be" UK's best "big man" since Spivey.

"At least he has the potential to be as good as any of the big men we've had," Lancaster said. "He's big enough, strong, fast, and quick.

"He's also aggressive, highly intelligent, and very mature for his age, even though he just turned 18 [November 1]."

"Lot of Work to Do"

Issel sat at courtside before a recent practice session and discussed his basketball future, which begins, for the record, here December 3, when the talented Kittens meet Cincinnati's freshmen in a preliminary to UK's opener with Virginia.

"Of course, anybody who plays under coach Rupp has in the back of his mind that he wants to be an All-American," Issel said. "And if I develop and if I'm good enough, I'd like to play pro ball.

"But after scrimmaging coach Rupp's varsity, you find that you still have a lot of work to do."

Issel thinks his biggest weakness is failure to get good rebounding position.

"In high school, I could outjump them, no matter where I was," he said, "but in college, you have to get good position."

His strengths were described by Art Laib, 6'9" transfer from Gulf Coast Junior College in Panama City, Florida. Laib has been working out with the freshman team and scrimmaging against Issel.

"He's a strong rebounder, and when he gets the ball inside, he's a good scorer because he's strong," Laib said. "He's quick for his size and real smart—knows what to do."

An accounting major who is one of the few basketball freshmen winning their battle with the books so far, Issel picked UK from "about 100 or 110" college offers because of UK's "fine basketball background."

He averaged 25 points and 18 rebounds as a high school senior, which earned him mention to All-State and All-America teams.

Does he like UK so far?

"Real well," he replied. "So far, it's everything they said it would be."

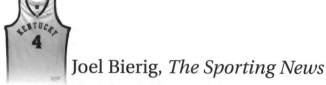

Joel Bierig, *The Sporting News*

MACY'S MAGIC

Kyle Macy, the prototypical "coach on the floor," helped lead Kentucky to a national title as a sophomore and became a Big Blue icon. When the school celebrated its 100th year of basketball in 2003, Macy was named to the five-man all-century team. The Sporting News ran this feature on the Cats leader during his 1978–80 senior season.

It was the afternoon before Kentucky would face Indiana, at that time the top-ranked college basketball team in the nation. Kentucky coach Joe Hall called his players to midcourt and began giving them a few last instructions. Finally he turned to one member of the group and said, "Do you have anything to add to that, Kyle?"

Kyle Macy is that kind of player.

To hear Hall tell it, the 6'3" senior guard from Peru, Indiana, is the only person in the nation capable of threatening his job security. "He's like a coach on the floor," Hall said.

It should be noted, however, that Macy can execute the X's and O's as well as he can draw them. Take this season's Southeastern Conference game against Auburn. Kentucky, stricken by the blahs after beating Notre Dame a few days earlier, was on the verge of sending Auburn home with a victory. With 12 seconds left, the score was tied at 65–65 and Kentucky called timeout to set up a play that would have Macy taking the last shot.

The play failed to come off as diagrammed, but Kentucky still got the ball to Macy with a couple of seconds left. Without bothering to take aim, he fired from 25 feet.

Swish! Kentucky 67, Auburn 65.

Afterward, Hall failed to share the fans' euphoria. "We missed eight layups in the first half," the coach said dourly. "We shot 31 percent. We had no defense, no rebounding. Kyle Macy managed the main chores and took charge when he had to."

Kyle Macy, you see, is that kind of player.

As Auburn coach Sonny Smith lamented afterward, "I don't think we made a mistake that beat us. I think we were beaten by a great player."

The player to whom Smith referred is not exceptionally big. He is not exceptionally quick. He is merely exceptional. Kyle Macy, a quiet, clean-cut kid who wears his hair short, is the player you would want to set up the last play, to take the last shot, to fling the final free throw.

In two consecutive games—a 61–60 victory over Purdue and an 86–80 triumph over Notre Dame—Macy was named most valuable player. No such honor was bestowed after the Auburn game, but it didn't matter. The passing out of ballots would have cut unnecessarily into the nation's paper supply.

"I really enjoy watching him play," says Bobby Knight, the rigid tactician who coaches Indiana. "I think it takes somebody who really understands the game to have a true appreciation of Macy."

Knight's appreciation of Macy blossomed last summer in San Juan, Puerto Rico, when they were united on the U.S. team in the Pan-American Games.

It was there that Macy suffered the biggest blow of his basketball career. The blow was a literal one, delivered from Macy's blind side by Tomás Herrera, a guard on the Cuban team.

"It was a deliberate punch," said Macy, who is hardly an expert on pugilism. It left him with a broken jaw and serious doubt about the justice of international competition. The U.S. Olympic Committee charged that it was the second time Herrera had been involved in an altercation with an American player in the last six years. Nevertheless, although Herrera was ejected from the game, he was not banned from further competition.

"The thing that bothers me most," says the usually soft-spoken Macy, "is the lack of support from our committee. You give up your summer and dedicate yourself to playing for your country, and then something like that happens. It has no place in basketball. It's uncalled for."

Says Macy's father, Robert, a spectator that night, "I'm disappointed to think somebody would do something like that. Had it hit him in the cheekbone or the eye, it could have been disastrous."

Robert Macy's concern was shared throughout the Bluegrass. As Kyle spent five weeks sipping his meals through a straw, Kentucky fans wondered whether his jaw—and his psyche—would ever heal sufficiently.

Their worries were for naught. So far, Macy has been the same cool customer he always has been, as good or better than the guy who was a sophomore playmaker on Kentucky's national title team in 1978, who led a struggling young team to a 19–12 record and a berth in the National Invitation Tourney last year. In Kentucky's first 13 games this season, Macy attempted 32 free throws. Only one missed its destination.

Nevertheless, statistics say little more about Macy than he does about himself. His scoring average—15.2 last year and about the same this season—does not reflect his worth. Suffice it to say that Knight, who failed to pursue Macy in high school, admits to "the biggest recruiting mistake I've ever made."

One day last summer, during practice for the Pan Am Games, Knight watched Macy shoot free throws in Indiana University's Assembly Hall. "If I wasn't such a dumb SOB," Knight told him, "you would have played your entire college career right here in this building."

Macy was Indiana's Mr. Basketball as a senior, averaging 35 points per game for a Peru High team coached by his father.

"They talked to me some," Macy said of IU, "but the first day they could sign people, they signed Bob Bender, who now is at Duke. They also had Quinn Buckner, Bobby Wilkerson, and Jim Wisman. I figured they already had enough guards."

It wasn't a case of a boy's dreams getting shattered. "I don't know if I had a favorite school," Macy said. In truth, however, his heart belonged to Indiana Tech, the school in Fort Wayne where his father used to coach.

"That was my favorite when I was small," Macy said. "I was the mascot for the team and used to put on halftime shows."

When the time came to pledge his allegiance, Macy opted for Purdue. On the surface, it appeared as if he had made a good choice. As a freshman he was third on the team in scoring (13.8), first in free-throw percentage (85.9), and second in assists (88). At the end of a 16–11 season with the Boilermakers, however, Macy felt empty and unaccomplished.

"Team play is a big part of basketball," he said. "I didn't see that being played, and I didn't see much prospect for it in the future."

So he packed his bag and headed for Kentucky, where the door always is open to any player willing to put the team ahead of himself. As soon as he announced his decision, Purdue fans began writing him nasty letters.

"I got a lot of bad mail when I left the school," Macy said. "People said a lot of bad things about me."

Imagine his delight, then, after Kentucky edged Purdue this season in the final of the UK Invitational. Before the game, the spotlight had focused on the big men—Sam Bowie of Kentucky and Joe Barry Carroll of Purdue. In the end, however, the center of attention did not stand 7'1", as had been advertised.

He towered 6'3".

Kyle Macy, held to four points in the first half, was indomitable after intermission. He hit five of six shots, scored 14 points, and knocked the ball away from Purdue's Keith Edmonson at the final buzzer.

For the record, Kyle Macy does not revel in rivalries. For three years now, reporters have tried to get him to say a few unkind words about Knight and Indiana. They might as well have been talking to Calvin Coolidge.

Moments after beating Purdue, however, the iceman melted: "The competitive nature in me tells me that if people say I can't do something, I'm going to try to prove them wrong," Macy said.

It was easier to talk about it as he sat on the Kentucky bench and waited for the all-tournament team to be announced. Moments later, he would hear his name called as the MVP. So, painfully, would every Purdue fan in the Rupp Arena crowd of 23,768.

"It's a completely different team, a completely different coaching staff," Macy said, noting that Lee Rose has taken over for Fred Schaus. "But the fans are still the same."

And many of them never understood why he left.

"It's kind of a tough decision when you decide to transfer," Macy said. "A lot of people think it's because you couldn't make it, that you're stepping down."

Basketball people knew better. In fact, the Phoenix Suns asked him to step up to the NBA when they drafted him in the first round last June. Although he was flattered to be chosen by Phoenix—"They play team ball," he noted—Macy never thought about foregoing his final year of college.

At the moment, he dreams of the day when Hall, accepting another national championship trophy, steps down from the podium at Market Square Arena in Indianapolis and says, "Do you have anything to add to that, Kyle?"

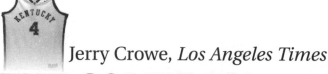

Jerry Crowe, *Los Angeles Times*

THE COMEBACK OF SAM BOWIE

Perhaps no Wildcat went through as much frustration during his career as 7'1" Sam Bowie. The classy Pennsylvania native endured and led Kentucky to the 1984 Final Four as a senior. The Los Angeles Times *chronicled Bowie's challenges early in his final UK season.*

A T-shirt hanging in the gift shop at the Campbell House Inn shows a Kentucky Wildcat and a Louisville Cardinal fighting for a basketball above the words "Play It Again, Sam."

The words have become a rallying cry in this basketball-mad city.

Sam Bowie, after missing two seasons with a slow-healing shin-bone injury that finally required bone-graft surgery, is being asked to recapture his past.

The fifth-year senior from Lebanon, Pennsylvania, who was the National High School Coaches Association Player of the Year in the same year that Ralph Sampson was a high school senior and who compared favorably with the former Virginia All-American in his first two years at Kentucky, is expected not only to regain his old form but also to lead the Wildcats to the NCAA championship.

"The fan expectation is enormous around here," the 7'1", 235-pound Bowie says matter-of-factly.

But Bowie has given indications that the fans who fill 23,500-seat Rupp Arena—Kentucky has led the nation in attendance since 1976—are not being unrealistic.

Although his contributions have not been as noticeable (his averages of 7.8 points and 8.0 rebounds a game through six games this season are down from his sophomore numbers of 17.4 and 9.1), some people say Bowie is all the way back.

One is Bowie himself, "I think I'm 100 percent mentally and physically," he said. "It's just that I'm playing a different role this year, and a lot of times when you look at the box scores, you're not going to see that many points from me."

Another is Marty Blake, director of scouting for the NBA, who calls Bowie "the consummate team player." He says that if none of a select few undergraduates make themselves available, Bowie will be one of the first two players chosen next spring in the NBA draft.

"He's made a remarkable recovery," Blake said.

Others, including Kentucky coach Joe B. Hall, are more cautious: "I don't think a player can come back after two years and be 100 percent in one year." But the consensus is that Bowie, whose shooting has been the worst part of his game, will eventually return to form, if he hasn't already. His shooting will come around, they say, as he plays himself into shape.

"I can see a great deal of improvement since the start of the season," Hall said last weekend after Bowie scored 28 points (11 for 18) and grabbed 21 rebounds in wins over Wyoming and BYU.

Bowie says he is "kind of glad" that he went through the ordeal of a two-year recovery from his broken left tibia, which required electrical stimulation, bone grafting, and at least five separate casts. He now wears a kneepad on his left shin.

"It was a learning experience for me," he said. "It gave me an opportunity to change my priorities in life. It's given me a different perspective."

When he was in the hospital, he said, he got a call from a young boy on another floor who was worried about Bowie's leg. Bowie climbed a flight of stairs on his crutches and made his way to a room where he found a boy whose cancer-ridden legs had been amputated.

Things like that do wonders for your perspective.

Bowie began feeling discomfort in his left leg in the summer of 1981. The previous summer, following his freshman year at Kentucky, he had been the standout of the U.S. Olympic team in a series of games against teams of NBA all-stars. But as he prepared for his junior year, pain shot through his leg when he jumped.

After first dismissing the injury as shin splints, doctors eventually took X-rays. They discovered a stress fracture of the tibia, the main weight-bearing bone in the lower leg. Bowie and his doctors have since looked at tapes of his games to find out how and when he was injured but have found nothing.

He was fitted for his first cast in the fall of 1981 and decided to sit out the 1981–82 season to retain two years of eligibility. But despite this conservative approach, the leg failed to heal properly. A year later, when it still hadn't healed, Bowie tried treatment that involved electrical stimulation. When that didn't work, he reluctantly agreed to the bone-graft surgery, in which bone chips from his pelvic area were used to fuse the fracture.

Although it was a frustrating period—his doctors never told him he would be able to play—Bowie said he never doubted that he would play again.

He had already been through what he considered a greater ordeal. His father, Ben, 45, a former player for the Harlem Magicians, had died of a ruptured cyst in the lung. Bowie is close to his family—when his younger sister was recovering from surgery, he held a press conference in her hospital room to announce his signing with Kentucky—and the loss of his father affected him deeply.

"Instead of asking myself why my leg was fractured," he said, "I was asking why my father had died."

Of the injury, he said: "I always approached it from the standpoint that I had a broken leg and one day it would heal. I knew it wasn't going to be 20 years; I knew it wasn't going to be forever. I was only 19 or 20 years old at the time and I knew I had nothing but time on my hands."

Bowie, born 22 years ago on St. Patrick's Day, concentrated on his studies during his time of inactivity. He has completed work toward a degree in organizational communications and begins taking graduate classes next month.

An outgoing person who says his time away from the game enabled him to show that Kentucky basketball players are "not just jocks," Bowie seems to enjoy his teammates and the adulation that goes with being a basketball player at Kentucky. But sometimes he wishes he were somebody else.

"I want to be just like the average 22-year-old kid," he said.

When it became apparent that Bowie would return this year, Kentucky's sports information department hailed him as a Player of the Year candidate. Hall asked for patience from the fans, who expected Bowie to lead the Wildcats to the national championship, but put him into the starting lineup.

His first game back was a nightmare. In an exhibition against the Netherlands' national team, an obviously nervous Bowie had four points and four turnovers in 20 minutes. Not like the Bowie who, in his first college game, had 27 points and 17 rebounds against Duke's Mike Gminski.

The critics were harsh.

"Sam's got a long way to go," said Hall, adding that Bowie was "40 percent of what he ought to be."

Wrote D.G. FitzMaurice in the *Lexington Herald-Leader*: "Absence may make the heart grow fonder, but it sure plays hell with one's basketball skills."

The most discouraged of all was Bowie.

"This is without a doubt the worst I've played," he told the *Herald-Leader*. "I know my teammates and friends are saying I did all right. Well, Sam knows the game of basketball. Sam knows when Sam has played well. Sam knows when Sam plays bad. Let's face it: I didn't get anything done."

Bowie, who hopes to play in the Olympics next summer, knew how far he had to come back.

"I found myself working at the things that ordinarily would have just come for granted," Bowie said. "I was blessed with so much God-given ability that I really didn't have to work as hard as the average individual [before the injury] because I was so talented. Now that I've been out for two years, I've got to work hard just to get back what I've lost."

Complicating matters, Bowie's role had changed. Instead of playing center and being the focal point of the offense, he found himself playing away from the basket as a forward. It's a position he had always said he wanted to play—at one point, he said, he and Sampson had decided to both play at Kentucky—but it was an adjustment just the same.

And although Kentucky always fields strong teams—the Wildcats are college basketball's winningest team over the last 50 years—Bowie is now part of a potentially great team. The NBA's Blake calls the unbeaten Wildcats "as strong as any college team I've seen as far as their first seven players go" and says six Kentucky players are potential first-round draft choices. One is 6'11" center Melvin Turpin.

"I'm not asked to do that much offensively," Bowie said. "Two years ago, I was getting the ball 15 or 20 times a game, but this year I'm getting it only five or six. About 90 percent of the time I get the ball, my responsibility is to get the ball down low to Melvin."

Not that Bowie isn't contributing.

He's shooting only 44.4 percent and averaging only six shots a game (compared to the 12 he averaged as a sophomore), but he leads the Wildcats in rebounding and is number two in assists. He handles the ball a lot at the high post and helps break the press. On defense, he overplays his man and denies the entry pass but still leads the team in blocked shots.

His shooting problems are the result of shooting without jumping for two years, but his shot will eventually come around, Bowie said. He has hit better than 50 percent in his last four games.

"I think Sam Bowie's game is emphasized in a lot of areas that don't show up in the statistics," Wyoming coach Jim Brandenburg said last Friday night after Bowie contributed 13 points and seven rebounds to a 66–40 win over his Cowboys. "His offensive rebounding and his ability to get to the ball so quickly cause people all kinds of problems. And his height and his long arms create all kinds of passing angles along the baseline. Defensively, when he gets his arms spread, he really cuts off a lot of passing lanes."

More importantly, Bowie is running and jumping freely. He fell hard to the floor after being fouled on an attempted dunk against BYU but bounced back up quickly.

And he seems to be enjoying himself.

"I find myself very pleased and very happy, even after only getting three shots against Louisville," Bowie told Ish Haley of the *Dallas Times Herald*. "Going back two years ago, I don't know if I would have had the same feelings or the same thoughts after a game."

He appreciates things a lot more.

And Kentuckians appreciate him. When Bowie announced at a press conference last December that he would return to Kentucky for a fifth year, the normally staid Hall hugged him.

Play it again, Sam.

Malcolm Moran, *The New York Times*

THE FRUSTRATION ENDS FOR BEAL

A teammate of Sam Bowie's, Dicky Beal was the glue that held the 1984 Cats together. Despite the words of Joe B. Hall—"He's going to wind up an immortal here at Kentucky"—Beal is often unsung when his team is remembered. Respected writer Malcolm Moran gave the diminutive Beal his due prior to the 1984 Final Four.

The white cord that had once been attached to a rim at Rupp Arena was now hanging around Dicky Beal's neck, and a light brown elastic bandage dangled from his right knee.

Over and over, Beal would try to satisfy the demands that are immediately placed on members of a championship team, to interpret and describe the feelings that had only arrived a few minutes before.

Again and again, he talked of the pain that had been replaced by the excitement of defeating Illinois in the Mideast Regional final to reach the Final Four of the national collegiate championship tournament. Beal remembered the frustration caused by the pain in his knee and the sting of the critics who examine Kentucky basketball as no other team is studied.

He remembered the end of the game, when he hugged the teammates, friends, and relatives who had helped him through the times when Beal thought his contributions were finished before his senior year was complete. "I just almost cried when I was going around, hugging people," Beal remembered. "People who stuck with me. I can look them in the eye today. They realize what you've been through and how hard it is to get there."

Saved His Name for Last

He recalled the announcement of the all-tournament team, when his name was not among the first four called. The reason Beal was not included was because his name had been saved for last as the outstanding player of the tournament. For all the talent and size the Kentucky program can attract, it was a 5'11" guard with an average of

6.2 points per game that pushed the Wildcats into the Final Four for the first time in six years. His pushing had helped him become the outstanding player.

"It's something I thought would never happen," he said.

And as Beal stood near his locker and all these new feelings stirred inside, he was reminded of a more basic sensation that has been with him for some time.

"I've got to sit down," he said.

Last August, the month before his 21st birthday and the start of his senior year, Beal underwent arthroscopic surgery, his third operation. Even now, Beal heats the knee for about 15 minutes before each practice and ices it for about 20 minutes afterward.

More Problems Than Bowie

"But it's holding up," Beal said. "It's really feeling good."

A short while later, it was obvious that the improvement in his knee is relative. "It always hurts me," Beal said. "I've just got to put it out of my mind now."

Joe B. Hall, the Kentucky coach, said that Beal has overcome more problems than even Sam Bowie, the Kentucky senior who missed two seasons with a stress fracture of his left shin bone and has still not fully recovered. "He's had everything spread through his career that you could have," Hall said of Beal. "No one has fought through more hardships."

He played behind Dirk Minniefield in his first three seasons, starting once as a sophomore, once as a junior, and just eight times in all. As a senior Beal did not become a starter until the game against Vanderbilt on February 19, the 23rd of the Kentucky season. He has started every game since.

His first important contribution came two games before Beal's first start, when he came off the bench to score 17 points against Auburn. In the 13 games since that afternoon, Beal has averaged 10.1 points and 7.3 assists. He has made 60.3 percent of his field-goal attempts and 78.7 percent of his free throws.

Somebody Had to Jump

The most important contribution, however, cannot be measured in numbers. Beal has added energy and enthusiasm to a team that has lacked those ingredients in recent years. For whatever reasons, whether the players had quiet personalities or the pressured atmosphere stifles any outward emotion, some of Kentucky's proudest moments have taken on a grim appearance.

"I thought we needed somebody out there that can jump up and down and say, 'Hey, it's not over,'" Beal said. "When there's five minutes left, jump up and down and say, 'Just five to go.' Then with two minutes, 'Just two to go.' It's something that we needed.

"The little man, you've got to be that way," Beal said. "You can't rebound, you can't block the big man's shots. You've got to do something else. That's my role, to get us fired up."

Beal just took over. When a teammate complains that he does not have the ball often enough, Beal answers sometimes less than diplomatically that there are others to consider. That leadership was difficult to perform earlier when the rehabilitation was not going smoothly. "Certainly, you don't feel like going out there and telling Sam Bowie or Mel Turpin where to go when you're in that shape," Hall said.

Earlier this season, when Beal's knee was responding slowly, the enthusiasm and leadership he could offer was fastened to the Kentucky bench. "I was telling people, 'Heck, it's over. I can't come back,'" Beal said.

"I was doubtful he was going to make any contribution at all many, many times," Hall said.

Those times now seem long ago. "Things change," Beal said. "My knee got better. Here I am today."

When Beal starts next Saturday in the national semifinals, it will be his 19th start out of his 110 games at Kentucky. The numbers are less important here than the fact that the Wildcats will be there, and the knowledge of how Beal pushed them all the way to Seattle.

"He's going to wind up an immortal here at Kentucky," said Joe B. Hall, who does not say such things very often.

Rick Bozich, *The* (Louisville) *Courier-Journal*

CRY OF THE CAT: A DAY OF HAPPY-NESS FOR WALKER

Senior Day is special, especially at Kentucky, and especially when former Governor Happy Chandler would sing "My Old Kentucky Home." Longtime Louisville Courier-Journal *columnist Rick Bozich ties together young (Kenny Walker) and old (Chandler) in this recap of Walker's last home game in 1986.*

For two seasons Kenny Walker has energetically ducked pounding forearms, collapsing triple teams, and every other defensive gimmick you can sketch on a chalk board. The only time the guy gets checked straight up is passing through airport metal detectors.

The regular-season version of Walker's robust University of Kentucky career ended yesterday. But before it did, there came a time when Walker might have found comfort in a crowd of four mugging opponents.

Here was A.B. "Happy" Chandler, the ageless former Kentucky governor, standing at center court in Rupp Arena, roaring to the conclusion of "My Old Kentucky Home," and there was Kenneth Walker looking for somebody to embrace. Bodies swayed, emotions flashed, voices stuck, tears flowed.

Richard Madison, large, muscular, and all shook up himself, dabbed at his left eye with a sweatband he hurriedly removed from his left wrist.

After four years, 125 games, 96 victories, and 1,936 points, The Sky was finally falling on Kenny Walker's UK basketball career.

And the kid—memories, joy, and regrets tearing across his long, naked face—wasn't doing so well himself.

"When I looked out there," said Madison, "you could tell it was really getting to Kenny. He looked like he was reaching out to the crowd."

Walker found Chandler, ever irrepressible, who wrapped his left hand firmly around Walker's thick neck and pulled him down safely underneath the relentless roar. Happy never turns anybody loose without a few words of wisdom.

"I just told him what I tell everybody I see," said Chandler. "I've watched basketball around here for more than 70 years and I've never seen anybody who played with his effort every night. I told him I'd really enjoyed that, and that I would miss him."

And Walker's emotions?

"He was crying," said Chandler. "I was crying. The other players were crying. Everybody was crying. Weren't you crying?"

For four years Walker's boundless determination has been one skill that's separated him from ordinary talents. Kenny Walker, the Backboard Stalker. Some guys can match his outside shot or vertical jump; nobody can match his perpetual scowl or flaming eyes. Sleep-Walker is the one thing he's never been tagged.

Emotional tank empty, tears still drying against his face, Kenny Walker simply played yesterday. His good-bye statement was strong and succinct: 17 points, five boards, three blocks, two steals, and two assists.

Watch him close out a three-pass fast break with a lob-dunk off Roger Harden's feed. Watch him chase LSU's John Williams to the bench with eight points, four fouls, and no satisfaction.

And, hey, there's the guy known for his tireless banging parked on the perimeter, stroking that 18-foot jumper. Twice.

Make a note of that, Ed Badger, front-row observer and representative of the Boston Celtics, who own an NBA lottery pick and the possible dream of selecting Walker.

"A lot of people think I can't shoot from outside," said Walker, smiling like a kid possessing a deep, delightful secret. "I hope teams keep playing me that way so I can stroke it the way I did today."

And then after he proved he can stroke it as easily as he smokes it, Walker retreated to the bench for the final 30 seconds, drinking in the adulation and dabbing at his tears.

"It's a feeling," said Walker, "that you can cherish for the rest of your life."

Tributes?

Let's start with Kentucky's 26–3 record in a year when nobody outside the locker room was suggesting a Southeastern Conference title or a Top 10 finish.

No wonder Louisiana State coach Dale Brown visited the UK bench to pump Walker's hand. That's a first for Dale Brown, not for Kenny Walker.

"I wanted to congratulate Walker because he is a special kind of player," said Dale Brown. "He is perpetual motion, the John Havlicek of college basketball. I don't think there is a player in the country that out-hustles Walker."

Memories?

"Five or 10 years from now it won't be the basketball stuff I remember," said Roger Harden, another senior who waved farewell. "I'll just remember rooming with him as a freshman and watching him grow into just a tremendous person."

Legacies?

"I'll just remember the example he set for the team," said Madison, the kid most likely to replace Walker next season. "The guy's an All-American. He doesn't have to come out and play and practice as hard as he does every night."

A grin from Madison.

"But he does. And he enjoys doing it."

Kentucky coach Eddie Sutton has climbed onto his ball rack lately to stump for Walker as Player of the Year over Len Bias, Walter Berry, Brad Daugherty, Steve Alford, Scott Skiles, and many others. In a season when the platform to number one has been a short plank and none of the dominant players scratch 7', there are nominees from every campus.

How can you separate them?

Why do you have to?

With or without the Rupp, Naismith, or Wooden awards, Kenny Walker's Ol' Kentucky legacy was indelibly scorched into Wildcat memories long ago.

He leads the country in skinned knees, bruised elbows, and scratched corneas. Imagine Pete Rose in short pants or Walter Payton in sneakers. Walker says the athlete he admires most is John McEnroe. He means his spirit, not his mouth. It shows.

Sutton can recite all of Walker's wonderful numbers from now until Dallas, but there's no need for politicking. Sutton's ultimate tribute came when he decided to hitch this team's future to the broad backs of Walker and Winston Bennett and play without a center.

Too small?

Not yesterday. Not all season.

Pounding the ball to Bennett (eight points) and Walker (a rumbling three-point play), Kentucky scored 15 of the second half's first 21 points. LSU never again moved closer than four, and UK became the first SEC team in five years to win 17 of 18 conference games.

And so when the time came for good-bye, Walker did not need to utter a word. But, hey, Kenny, how would you like to be remembered?

"I don't want to be remembered as a great scorer or a great rebounder or a great shot blocker," said Walker. "I want to be remembered as a complete basketball player who gave 110 percent every time he went on the court."

And, just as Happy Chandler told him, that will not be a problem.

John McGill, *The Sporting News*

CHAPMAN, BASKETBALL INSEPARABLE

Already a Kentucky high school phenom before arriving in Lexington in late 1986, King Rex took the commonwealth by storm as a Wildcat fresh-man. The Sporting News *ran this feature on Rex Chapman just two months into his college playing career.*

The first lime Rex Chapman met his destiny, which happens to be bas-ketball, he was two years old.

It happened during a Kentucky Colonels game in the old American Basketball Association. The year was 1969. The Colonels had just called a timeout. As Wayne Chapman joined his teammates in the huddle, his son Rex embarked on a journey.

It seems the referee had placed the ball on the court. Leaving his mother Laura behind, out from the stands waddled Rex Chapman, two, drawn to the ball like a moth to a flame. Before the referee noticed what was happening, Rex had grabbed the ball.

"I didn't see him do it," Wayne Chapman recalled with a laugh, "but I heard the commotion. And when I looked up from the huddle, I saw them taking him off the court. He didn't have the ball then, but Laura said that when they came after him, he started running away with it."

In the years since, it has become increasingly difficult to separate Rex from the basketball.

Chapman, a sophomore, led the University of Kentucky in scoring with 18.4 points entering the Wildcats' game with Tennessee January 16. As a freshman he led the team in scoring with an average of 16 points per game.

You might think that Chapman's ascension into hoop heaven was a result of his father's prodding and influence. After playing on the freshman team at Kentucky, Wayne Chapman transferred to Western Kentucky, where he was an All-Ohio Valley Conference selection three straight years. Then he spent three years in the ABA before a back injury ended his playing career. Now he's the head coach at NCAA Division II power Kentucky Wesleyan in Owensboro.

"He wouldn't know what to do if he wasn't around basketball," Rex said.

But both father and son say that Rex's love affair with the sport was a result of the youngster's natural inclination, not the father's dream. Just as the toddler once decided to pursue a ball, the teenager decided to embrace the game.

"I just played for myself. I just wanted to be a basketball player because it's something I enjoy," Rex said. "If I wanted to ask my dad something about the game, I'd go to him. But he didn't volunteer information."

"I guess it was osmosis more than anything," Wayne said, "It wasn't one of those father-son situations where we battled back and forth on the idea. He made the decision and developed his talents."

It might surprise you to learn, for instance, that as Rex began to mature, there was no basketball goal in the Chapman driveway.

"I never wanted one," Rex said.

"That's true," Wayne said. "But he always had a gym to go to. And you've got to realize that in the city of Owensboro, there's one basket for every two houses. Rex would get up in the morning, get on his bike with a ball under his arm, and either find a game or just shoot on his own. He'd show up for dinner—sometimes."

There was a time when Rex did have his own basket. He was just too young to remember.

"He had one when he was born," Wayne said. "We got a regular-size goal and attached it to a telephone pole with a couple of bolts. At the age of two, he was tall enough to pick up the ball, carry it over, and drop it in the basket. It was set so low he'd have to pick up the net and get the ball out from under it.

"As he kept growing, we kept moving it up. At three, he was shooting up to six feet. At four and a half, he was shooting at a 10-foot goal."

By the time he was 12, Chapman twice had been named to all-star teams in both Pop Warner football, in which be was a quarterback, and Little League baseball, in which be was a pitcher. But it was about this time that Rex told his parents that he was going to forget those sports and concentrate on basketball.

Wayne Chapman was not elated. The more sports you play, the more chances for an athletic scholarship down the road. What if Rex had a better chance to develop a great curveball than be did a jump shot?

"I'm looking at him, and he's about 5'4"," Wayne recalled. "I thought, 'This could be a hell of a mistake.' I asked him, 'Rex, what if you don't grow and don't get better?' He said, 'I will.' And he did."

"But it was a very scary moment, to be honest with you. I don't think it's a good thing for kids to concentrate on one sport at that age. My wife and I discussed it and considered discouraging him. But we decided that because he was good at academics, he was going to get an education anyway."

Meanwhile, Rex's basketball education continued to come easily. In 1978 Wayne Chapman was the coach at Apollo High in Owensboro. That Apollo team was ranked number one in Kentucky and was unbeaten until being upset by eventual state champion Shelby County in the first round of the state tourney.

Apollo had such players as Jeff Jones, later a starter at Virginia, and Steve Barker, who became the career scoring leader at Samford. Rex, 11 at the time, would shoot at one end of the gym while Apollo practiced at the other.

"Rex was fortunate because he had an exceptional team to watch," Wayne said. "And he'd watch them every day. He saw what they were doing, and he began to do it himself—passes between the legs and behind the back. He was doing difficult things even before he realized how difficult they were."

Father and son rarely played against each other.

"No," Rex said. "As soon as Dad quit as a player, he was through."

"We'd prank around every once in a while, but nothing serious," Wayne said, "I didn't want to do that because either he wanted to play on his own or he didn't."

By the time Rex was ready to play high school ball, his father had moved across town from Apollo High to Wesleyan. Chapman averaged 27.2 points per game as a junior and 25.6 as a senior, becoming the state's "Mr. Basketball" in the process.

Through it all, Wayne Chapman did little more than monitor his son's progress.

"The main thing he always said was that I should play as hard as I could and that I should learn the difference between good and great," Rex said. "A lot of good players have the ability, but they don't really work to improve."

And when did Rex learn that?

"It took getting to college to realize it, because in high school most players didn't have as much ability as I had," he said. "I always heard my dad saying it, and I always tried to play hard. But you don't realize what playing hard is until you get to college."

Rex and Wayne talk on the phone two or three times a week. Rex may be too young to remember much about his father's playing career, but check Kentucky's media guide for the athlete he most admires: Wayne Chapman.

Sons of coaches usually play well because they pick up the game's nuances at an early age. In Chapman's case, however, you can add uncommon talent to the equation.

But it is his love for the game, not any desire to eclipse his father's accomplishments, that has put him where he is today.

"Rex was too young to realize much when I was playing ball," Wayne said, "but he could sense the excitement at a pro game."

That is why, of course, Rex Chapman, 20, came up with his first steal on a basketball court 18 years ago.

Michael Bradley, *The Sporting News*

MASH BASH

Kentucky's return to basketball supremacy was kick-started when Jamal Mashburn decided to wear the Blue and White. After helping the Unforgettables get to the brink of the Final Four in 1992, Mashburn led the Wildcats to the promised land a year later. The Sporting News highlighted the All-American prior to UK's 1992–93 season.

The drill begins with a curious ritual that resembles an initiation rite of sorts. Ten young men, arms held aloft, run silently in a tight ring around the free throw circle inside the University of Kentucky's Memorial Coliseum. Each wears a look of anticipation, knowing he is about to be tested.

In an instant, a shot is launched and the circle breaks. The ceremonial follow-the-leader game dissolves into a full-court scrimmage. Big people head for the backboard and the ball, and the smaller ones scurry around the perimeter. Kentucky basketball practice is back in session.

As Coach Rick Pitino shouts for meticulous operation of his patterned offense, the 10 young men struggle to impress. Four seniors are gone from last season's team, so there is plenty of opportunity. Pitino is waiting.

Another shot goes awry, and junior forward Jamal Mashburn grabs the rebound. He spins away from a teammate and starts up court, a 6'8", 240-pound one-man fast break. Take the charge? You had better have good medical coverage.

Just past midcourt, Mashburn assesses his situation. Three men back; no teammates alongside him. The options are clear: steamroller or retreat. He pulls back, bouncing the ball behind him to a trailer, point guard Travis Ford.

But Mashburn isn't done. So he didn't get the points right away. No problem. He runs through the lane and makes a quick right turn for the corner. Once there, Mashburn takes a pass from Ford and hits a three-point shot. Sweet. Mashburn's patience has paid off.

When Mashburn surrendered the ball like that during his first two seasons in Lexington, Kentucky, it might have been a result of his shyness and respect for his elders. To him, underclassmen had no right to demand the ball, to dominate the game. That distinction went to seniors. Forget the fact that his presence on a basketball court could earn him respect and the opportunity to lead. Mashburn stepped back. They called him the "Monster Mash," but he really was just a monster-in-training.

In his freshman season, he deferred to senior Reggie Hanson. Last season the spotlight belonged to "The Unforgettables," four seniors who stuck with Pitino through probation and ridicule. Mashburn didn't try to dominate and opponents were thankful.

But this season, it's his team. If he wants it. And when Mashburn gives up the ball on the break, he does so because he knows he'll get it back. He is option number one this season, a sterling combination of inside power and outside finesse. Mashburn likes the responsibility. "Give me the ball," he tells teammates. "And get out of the way."

Consider the training complete. Like a young warrior who submits to his elders' teaching and testing, Mashburn has evolved into a learned man. He is *the* man. Presenting…the real Monster Mash.

"I thought it was the seniors' team last year," says Mashburn, who turns 20 Sunday. "I was only a sophomore. It didn't look right. They were here longer than I was and I just felt it was their team and their time to shine.

"This year, it's my team."

Listen up, Southeastern Conference. Hear this, NCAA. The Mash has spoken. He shoots like an off-guard. He handles it like a man four inches shorter. He rebounds. He owns the low box. "There's not a guy in the NBA who readily comes to mind who does all that," Pitino says. Now that Mashburn's attitude finally is matching his physical promise, look out.

Of course, no one is happier with the metamorphosis than Pitino, the transplanted New Yorker who lured a pudgy, bashful Mashburn south from Harlem three years ago by promising to prepare him for pro ball. Well, Mash is just about ready. Pitino has helped transform the shy kid into a force. Mashburn gets credit, too, for trimming off the baby fat, working hard on his jump shot, and ignoring the head-spinning adulation heaped on him by Kentucky's adoring, somewhat single-minded fans.

But Pitino's mouth may have been the single most important catalyst in Mashburn's emergence. A two-year sermon from one of the all-time talkers has to have an effect. "Get more aggressive, Mash. Dominate, Mash. Be the man, Mash." Enough already.

"He's very persistent," Mashburn says. "It wears off on you, finally."

By the end of last season, Mashburn occasionally slipped on the leader's cloak, checking it out for size and comfort. And last summer, he was one of eight lucky college players selected as practice fodder for the U.S. Olympic team. Talk about your potential confidence-drainer. Put a 19-year-old on Karl Malone, and he'll most likely come back battered and bowed. Not so. Mashburn watched. He listened. He learned.

He saw Larry Bird lead by example and Charles Barkley by sheer force. He even learned from Chris Mullin that a cheeseburger is not jump shot food. By the time Mashburn got back from Portland, Oregon, his goal of being an NBA star had crystallized, and his intention to take charge at Kentucky was clear.

"The summer changed him tremendously," Pitino says. "He looks at his diet differently. He is now committed to being a great pro. He now wants to dominate a game. It was like a coming-out party for him.

"I think that right now it's an unspoken thing that Jamal has to have the ball, and that Jamal is the man. Everybody knows it."

So Massachusetts's John Calipari is the hot, young coach, is he? Boy Wonder. Pitino on training wheels. Let's talk strategy with the latest hoops genius.

Tell us, coach, how do you stop Jamal Mashburn?

"This tells you how dumb I am as a coach," Calipari says with a laugh. "When we played them last March, I told the team Mashburn couldn't beat us alone, so don't double-team him.

"So what happens? We go down by 21 in the first half, and he had 15. I changed to a double-team, and we got back into the game."

Philadelphia, late March 1992. Massachusetts brings its 30 victories and a resurgent program into the Spectrum for an Elite Eight battle against Mash and Kentucky. Former UMass star Julius Erving attends the game, which matches coaches with a similar appearance and style. Fans can't figure out if that's Pitino with the Minutemen and Calipari with the Wildcats. Or is Pitino with the Wildcats... "He's the one in the nicer suit," Calipari jokes.

No one, however, has a problem spotting Mashburn. Given the freedom to roam the floor with only one man on him, Mash scores 30 on 11-for-15 shooting in the Wildcats' 87–77 victory. A controversial technical foul called on Calipari for leaving the coach's box thwarts UMass's late charge, but Mashburn had decided the game much earlier. Freed from the junk defenses he saw in the Southeastern Conference—Florida played four guys around him in a game last season—Mashburn was unstoppable.

"He is the most powerful athlete we played against last year." Calipari says. "It's not even close."

It took a while before Mashburn made proper use of his powers. He had some big games last season, to be sure, and his numbers—21.3 points per game, 7.8 rebounds per game, 56.7 field-goal percentage—were outstanding. But that didn't stop Pitino from badgering him about being more aggressive. After the Wildcats lost to Arkansas, 105–88—in Lexington, no less—Pitino implored Mashburn to get meaner and to commit harder, I-mean-business fouls. When Kentucky dropped a 74–53 decision to Louisiana State a week later, Mashburn appeared intimidated by the Tigers' Shaquille O'Neal. Pitino was on him again after consecutive victories against Alabama and Western Kentucky.

Nag, nag, nag.

"When I was choosing a college, I felt I needed someone to push me," Mashburn says. "If I wanted to go to the NBA, I had to be more aggressive. Being around people like Coach Pitino rubs off on you. He is a motivational coach."

Mashburn came to Kentucky from Cardinal Hayes High School in the Bronx. He didn't make the McDonald's All-America team, and his house was not a must-stop on every recruiter's road map. But Pitino liked Mashburn's skills, particularly his ability to handle and shoot the ball—baby fat be damned. The kid wasn't lazy, just shy. Pitino convinced Mashburn to sign early and then had the pleasure of watching his recruit lead Hayes to the Catholic high school championship in New York City.

"When I wasn't picked for the [high school] All-America team, I decided I was going to take my team to the championship," Mashburn says.

When Mashburn arrived at Kentucky, Pitino could see he was lacking in confidence. It even came out in the psychological tests Kentucky gives its players. "He did not totally believe he was a great player," Pitino says. So, the work began. Mashburn's body-fat percentage dropped from 15 to eight, and he practiced putting more arc on his jumper. Mashburn started all 28 games as a freshman, averaging 12.7 points per game and seven rebounds per game, as Kentucky completed its NCAA probation. Thank you very much, Eddie Sutton.

Mashburn's numbers increased his sophomore season, but there was Pitino, in his ear, in his face, telling him he could be better. By the end of the season, it all finally stuck.

At halftime of the SEC championship game, the Wildcats trailed Alabama, 32–29. Pitino ripped the team in the locker room and walked out. Mashburn took over. He told his teammates to wake up, play hard, and get him the ball. "That was very untypical of Jamal," Pitino says. Mashburn finished with 28 points and 13 rebounds, and the Wildcats roared to an 80–54 victory.

"He's a good leader, a quiet leader," Kentucky senior guard Dale Brown says. "People may not know it, but we see it. He tells us when to pick it up."

By tournament time, Mashburn had taken charge. Though he wasn't on the floor for the thrilling finish in Kentucky's 104–103 overtime loss to Duke in the East Regional final—he fouled out in regulation—he collected 28 points and 10 rebounds. The message had been sent. The

Unforgettables may have been sentimental favorites, but Mashburn no longer was in awe of them.

"It had to be done," Mashburn says about his Alabama outburst. "I don't brag about it. I just go out and do it. I tell them to give me the ball and keep moving. Everything will work out. I feel comfortable being a leader.

"The game gels tight, and you have to take the last shot. I want to take the last shot every game. When everything's good, it's easy to be a leader. When everything's bad, that's when a leader takes over."

During a game last season, Georgia coach Hugh Durham became the basketball equivalent of Goldilocks. Faced with defending Mashburn and his dangerous inside-outside game, Durham tried seven-footer Charles Claxton on him.

Too big.

He switched to 6'10" Arlando Bennett.

Too slow.

He finished with 6'7" Mike Green.

Too small.

Mashburn finished with 26 points and seven rebounds in an 84–73 victory.

"I had to guard him for two possessions, and he took me outside," Claxton says. "I gave him a cushion, and he drained the three. I was yelling, 'Coach, coach, switch me.'"

Claxton isn't alone. Big people all over the SEC tried to beg off guarding Mashburn. Big people couldn't follow him around the perimeter, and forwards had trouble containing him inside. "He has the body of a power forward, the ball-handling skills of a guard, and inside ability of a low-post center," Vanderbilt coach Eddie Fogler says.

Beyond all that is Mashburn's predisposition toward the game's finer points. Sure, he may look like an offensive foul waiting to happen, but the guy actually thinks pass first. He doesn't want to be a point guard or anything—hear that, Ralph Sampson—but he does understand that a well-placed pass can be as effective as a powerful move through the defense.

"He kills you in a quiet way," says UMass forward Lou Roe. "He starts off slow, like a Michael Jordan. He gets everybody else in the game first. If things aren't going right, he starts to take over."

To understand Mashburn's ball-handling skills, we have to flash back to his days in the schoolyards in New York. Big people don't get the ball much in pickup games, so Mashburn had to improvise. "Basically, I decided that, 'Hey, I like to score, too. I just don't want to be out there,'" Mashburn says. "So I learned how to dribble."

And how to shoot. You have heard about big people with range, but Mashburn's jumper resembles that of a shooting guard. He shot 43.9

percent (58 for 132) from three-point range last season, a remarkable percentage for a player his size. Sure, Don MacLean nailed a lot of three-pointers, too, but could he do the Monster Mash inside? No chance.

Mashburn hit Vanderbilt for five three-point shots the second time they played last season, and he helped ruin South Carolina's SEC coming-out party with 33 points, including 5-for-15 shooting from three-point range. It's not every night that a guy that big shoots 15 three-pointers and is still in the lineup the next game.

"He does a good job shooting from the outside, and that makes it tough on big guys," Auburn forward Wesley Person says. "It's hard to hold a player like him down. You just try to contain him and not let him have a big game."

Pitino concedes that the increased attention on Mashburn this season may lower his output. "I don't think you'll see Jamal score 30 points a night," he says. And he won't have to. Pitino has surrounded Mashburn with top-flight talent such as Ford, Brown, junior-college transfer Rodney Dent, and heralded freshmen Tony Delk and Rodrick Rhodes. But Pitino and Durham concede that Kentucky is the SEC favorite for one reason: Mashburn.

"That means I'm up on every chalkboard as the man who has to be stopped," Mashburn says with a laugh.

It also means that the NBA beckons. Last summer in Portland, Mashburn learned that he could hang with the big boys. He and the other seven "Baby Dream Teamers" may have been the silver medalists in Barcelona.

"Being on the court with the pros is very physical, and they maintain a quick pace," Mashburn says. "You really have to go to the basket—no time for showboating. Two points count more than anything."

Because there is a thin senior class in the country this season, Mashburn likely would be among the top five players selected in the NBA draft—if he chooses to leave Kentucky. And though no one is saying for certain that this will be Mashburn's last season, there are some pretty revealing clues.

"It's time for him to come out," Pitino says. "He's mentally and physically ready. I told Jamal, 'Don't be typical of everybody.' Shaq comes out and says he's definitely playing four years. This guy comes out and says, 'I don't know.' Be honest with the media. Be honest with the fans. They'll all appreciate it."

Mashburn spent most of his first two seasons promising Kentucky fans that he would complete his eligibility in Lexington. Now, Mash isn't too sure. He tasted the professional life last summer, and he liked it. Nothing is certain, but this may be Mashburn's last season.

"He's a very talented player," says Barkley, who banged around with Mashburn during Dream Team practices. "He's going to be a very good NBA player. He has great legs, a great lower body, and very good offensive skills."

Malone agrees. "He has all the tools," he says.

This season, that collection of weapons includes confidence and a willingness to lead. Mashburn may not be free from Pitino's harangues, but he doesn't have to worry about deferring to the Unforgettables or Reggie Hanson anymore. The 1992–93 Kentucky Wildcats are his team, and Mashburn's mixture of physical skills and self-assurance may only be truly tested at the next level.

"I feel I can play with the NBA players," Mashburn says. "I feel I can play with anybody. That's the confidence I have. I was watching something yesterday [on TV] about Shaquille O'Neal, and I saw him holding up his jersey after being drafted number one. That still excited me.

"It's a dream of mine. And when dreams come true, it's kind of scary."

Particularly for opponents.

Coaching legend Adolph Rupp, shown here in 1960, won 879 games and four national titles at the helm of the Kentucky Wildcats.

Section IV
THE COACHES

Tev Laudeman, *The Rupp Years*

A FRESHMAN HELPS HIRE UK COACH, THEN PLAYS FOR HIM

Tev Laudeman's book The Rupp Years *is a chronological review of every season Adolph Rupp led Kentucky's basketball program. The first year, 1930–31, details how a talented young freshman, Ellis Johnson, helped his school select the man who would become the sport's winningest coach.*

If there had been anyone on the University of Kentucky athletic council with the gift of prophecy, he surely would have made high drama of a meeting the group held on a spring day in 1930.

Photographers, ringing phrases, and maybe even champagne all around wouldn't have been overdoing it if the council had known exactly what it was about to accomplish.

All members of the council knew, though, that this wasn't a routine meeting. They were going to interview, and possibly hire, a new basketball coach.

And the council was in an uncomfortable position. Many fans thought it had erred in not matching or bettering the offer Miami University (Ohio) had made in luring Coach Johnny Mauer from UK. After all, Mauer had taken over after a season in which UK had won only three games and produced three straight winners. His last team had won 16 of 19 games, and he had recruited brilliantly for the future.

One member of the athletic council represented the student body. He was only a freshman, and it was unusual for a first-year man to be on the council. But this youth was not an ordinary freshman. He had been a high school All-American in both football and basketball at Ashland, Kentucky, and was a star in baseball and track. He was the greatest athlete UK had ever landed.

The interview came off well. The freshman didn't just sit back and listen to his elders. He took an active part in the session.

When the meeting was over and the coach had departed, the members of the athletic council agreed they were impressed with the coach's manner and his refreshing approach to basketball. They reached the decision quickly: UK would hire the man.

That's how freshman Ellis Johnson helped hire his own coach, Adolph Frederick Rupp. Johnson went on to become a three-year starter and an All-American as a senior. Rupp would win more games than any other coach in college basketball history. It was truly a momentous day for the UK athletic council.

The announcement was made formally on May 21, 1930, that UK had signed the 29-year-old Rupp to a two-year contract as head basketball coach, freshman football coach, and assistant to Bernie Shively with the track team.

Born in Halstead, Kansas, on September 2, 1901, Rupp had been a senior guard on Dr. Forrest "Phog" Allen's undefeated University of Kansas team in 1923. Rupp's Freeport, Illinois, high school teams had won more than 80 percent of their games over a four-year period.

Ellis Johnson got a chance to talk more basketball with Rupp when they ran into one another on the campus. Johnson was delighted when Rupp told him of plans to install the fast break, a sharp contrast to the slow, meticulous offense run by Mauer.

Later Rupp sent for Carey Spicer, captain-elect of the basketball team. Spicer was curious but mildly apprehensive. An all-around athlete, Spicer was starting quarterback on the football team and a member of the tennis squad, although he admitted he played tennis "just to get out of spring football practice."

As a sophomore Spicer had been named an All-American in basketball under Mauer only two years after winning All-State honors at Lexington High School. Now, after two seasons with Mauer, Spicer was going to play his senior year under a strange coach. Is there any wonder he was troubled?

As he shook hands with Rupp, Spicer saw a man nearly equal his own 6'1" height, already a bit on the portly side, dark hair combed neatly in place. But the impact of the coach's personality was greater than his visual impression.

Rupp told Spicer that set patterns would be retained, but when possible UK would run, with more chance for individual initiative on the part of the players.

Rupp questioned Spicer carefully about the returning players. Spicer painted an encouraging picture. Paul McBrayer, the All-American guard, and Lawrence "Big" McGinnis were gone, but among those back were 6'4" George Yates and clever Louis "Little" McGinnis, along with such promising players from the freshman squad as 6'4" Forest "Aggie" Sale and rugged Ellis Johnson.

Both Spicer and Rupp were pleased with their first meeting. The coach now was certain he had the personnel to make the fast break work, and he liked Spicer's eager acceptance of the forthcoming changes. Spicer felt his misgivings vanish under the spell of Rupp's sales talk.

Six players were missing when Rupp called the first practice of the 1930–31 season. Spicer, Johnson, Yates, Jake Bronston, Darrell Darby, and Bud Cavana still were with the football squad. Spicer was adding luster to an already bright football career by scoring 75 points in his senior season, highest total in the state and the Southern Conference. Practice tempo picked up after the footballers reported.

On December 18, UK opened its schedule at home against nearby Georgetown College. On the first play of the game, Aggie Sale tipped the ball to Spicer, who threw it to Johnson under the basket. Johnson laid it in to become the first player to score for Rupp at UK.

UK won the game 67–19 as Sale, the lanky sophomore from Lawrenceburg, scored 19 points, and Louis McGinnis of Lexington hit 17. Other starters were Spicer, Johnson, and Bill Trott of Evansville, Indiana.

Lancaster Scores 10
Yates, the tall pivotman from Elizabethtown, came off the bench to get 10 points. Other UK players in action were Bronston, Vernon Congleton, Walter Crump, Allan "Doc" Lavin, George Skinner, Cecil Bell, Charles Worthington, Bill Kleiser, Ercel Little, and Cavana. Before the season was over, Bronston, from Lexington, and Worthington, from Louisville, would be starting.

Georgetown had little to offer in offensive punch except a husky guard, Harry Lancaster, better known for his halfbacking on the football team. He scored 10 points and played well on defense. Eighteen years later he would become Rupp's first full-time assistant.

By the middle of February, UK had won 10 straight. The toughest game was at Vanderbilt, where Spicer scored 27 points. The score was tied 18–18 at halftime. Rupp, who always wore a brown suit with brown socks and tie to the game for good luck, asked Jake Bronston, "What were you thinking out there?"

Bronston, who was having a miserable night, replied, "Coach, I was just wondering if you had on those brown socks." Kentucky won 42–37.

A 36–32 victory at Tennessee was costly, as Ellis Johnson suffered a sprained ankle and was ordered to the sidelines for at least two weeks.

If Rupp wasn't already 100 percent superstitious, he had reason to be after he took his 10-game winning streak to Georgia. UK was upset on Friday, February 13, 25–16. Chief Georgia weapons were a defense that smothered Carey Spicer (he got one point) and a forward named Bill Strickland, who hit three straight goals late in the game.

Making the loss embarrassing for Rupp, Georgia was coached that night by football coach Harry Mehre, filling in for Herman Stegeman, who was out of town.

Still stunned by its first defeat, UK bowed to Clemson 29–26, then closed the trip by defeating coach Roy Mundorff's Georgia Tech team 35-16. UK finished the season with a 12–2 record by returning home to beat Vanderbilt 43–23 a week before the Southern Conference tournament in Atlanta.

About 300 fans were at the railroad station to see UK off for Atlanta. Ellis Johnson was there, but only to say good-bye. Because of his ankle injury, Johnson had to yield his place on the tournament squad to Ercel Little.

Long Shot Beats UK

Rupp's starting team for the tourney was the same as it was for the last few games of the regular season: Carey Spicer and Louis McGinnis, forwards; George Yates, center; and Jake Bronston and Charles Worthington, guards.

UK beat North Carolina and Duke in the first two games, McGinnis getting 18 points against Duke. Carey Spicer put on a spectacular show as Florida was crushed 56–35, scoring 11 points in one two-minute stretch on his way to a 22-point total.

The championship game between UK and Maryland was one of the most exciting played in the South all season. With less than a minute to play, McGinnis hit from near the sideline to give UK a 27–25 edge, but Maryland came right back to tie the score on a layup by guard Bozzy Berger. Then, as the final seconds ticked off, Berger swished through a long shot to give Maryland the title, 29–27.

Back home, Rupp called spring practice for April 21. In the meantime, the coach wore painful blisters on his feet refereeing district high school tourney games. Louisville Manual won the state crown, and the play of a guard for the champs, Russell "Duke" Ellington, caught Rupp's eye. Next fall Ellington would enroll at UK.

Rupp's success in his first year at UK would be overshadowed by conference and national championships of later seasons. Yet it is doubtful if any of the years to follow were more important to his career.

He took over strange personnel, introduced a new style of play, and had the difficult task of following another successful coach.

So well did he blend his players and system of play that Carey Spicer, Louis McGinnis, George Yates, and Jake Bronston were named to the All-Southern squad, and Spicer was selected to an All-American team for the second time in three years. Under Rupp, Yates was able to fully develop an unorthodox backhand flip shot, which Mauer had discouraged.

"Rupp didn't care how you shot as long as you put the ball in the basket," Yates recalled years later. The tall center doubts that Aggie Sale would have been nearly as good under Mauer.

"Aggie would shoot off balance, falling down, or sitting on the floor if he had to," explained Yates. "Mauer wouldn't have permitted that."

All in all, you'd have to say that freshman on the athletic council helped hire the right man.

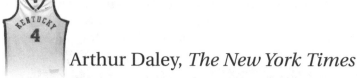

Arthur Daley, *The New York Times*

HIS OLD KENTUCKY HOME

This piece, the first of two selections from Arthur Daley of The New York Times *included here, quotes the Baron predicting increased popularity in the sport of basketball. This column appeared after UK played a pair of games in New York City in late December 1943.*

No more rabid enthusiast for the State of Kentucky exists than Adolph Rupp, a Kansas boy who traded in a Midwestern twang for a soft Southern drawl 14 years ago when he became the basketball coach at the University of Kentucky. He now has a true Chamber-of-Commerce outlook on life in Kaintuck and will recite the glories of the State at the slightest provocation.

Adolph was in town last week with his Wildcat court quintet. These visiting firemen have been wheeling in and out of New York so quickly of late that it has been difficult to catch up with most of them. He was nailed on the fly before his departure, a very happy gent because his operatives had just driven rugged St. John's from the ranks of the unbeaten.

They won without having to resort to Adolph's favorite stratagem, bringing his foemen on an extended pregame tour of the horse-breeding farms near Lexington.

"I finally got wise to him," said Doc Carlson of Pitt, sadly. "Adolph takes these kids from one farm to another on the afternoon of the game. First of all they are practically frozen to death by the time they have finished an exhausting tour. Then, as the grand finale, he takes them to see Man o' War.

A Horse Laugh from Big Red

"Adolph always makes a big concession on this part of the trip. He regularly arranges it so that the visiting players are permitted to touch the sacred skin of Big Red. This makes them feel that they will be lucky. But the truth of the matter is that Man o' War is a Kentucky horse and he never even bats an eye as he puts the jinx on them."

Mr. Rupp does not even bother to deny the allegation. Being an admirer of the Doc's and being always amused by his sallies, he merely laughs at him. "We're very proud of our breeding farms," he drawls. "In our county of Fayette alone we have $45 million worth of horse flesh. Naturally, I like to educate our visitors in the finer attributes of the great State of Kentucky." Kansas papers please copy.

Except for a couple of short side trips to neighboring centers, the Wildcats have completed their traveling for the season and no one is happier about it than Adolph Rupp. So far this campaign he's had a few far-from-delightful experiences.

"We left Lexington one day," he said, "and expected to have to ride by coach to Cincinnati. But the train was so jammed that we finally wound up in the baggage car. The boys sat around on mail sacks playing cards and actually seemed to enjoy it more than if they'd been in Pullmans.

"On another trip to Champaign to meet Illinois, we had to lay over and catch a train at 3:00 AM. I got the boys to bed early, awakened them in time, and down we went to the station. No train. We waited a bit and found that a derailing down the line had delayed it two hours. So back we went to the hotel for more sleep. At 5:00 we learned that the train wouldn't get in before 7:00. And at 7:00 they told us it wouldn't get in at all.

"Therefore, we compromised on a bus for the rest of the trip and the only food we had all day was what hot dogs we could get at roadside stands. Did these kids mind it? They did not. They sang all the way into Champaign and went out to play the very finest game they've produced all season."

Food for Thought

"Episodes like those make me wonder if we haven't been pampering our athletes too much with Pullmans, special diets, and the like. Maybe the recipe for winning basketball is baggage cars and hot dogs. Be that as it may, however, I've had more fun, less grief, and more satisfaction out of coaching this group of youngsters than I ever had before.

"On September 24 we decided to carry on with a varsity basketball team. We had only 270 civilians in school, of whom only three were known to have court experience. The call went out and the boys started rolling out of the Kentucky hills so that I wound up with a squad of ten 17-year-olds and two deferred sophomores. It's been such a successful experiment that I wouldn't be surprised if we and a lot of the other colleges which abandoned football resumed next season. I feel we owe it to the boys themselves."

It would have broken Adolph's heart if he had been shut out of coaching basketball this year. He hasn't been shut out in a couple of campaigns. The last one came when Kentucky visited Georgia Tech to dedicate a new arena there, a beautiful fireproof place which was the last word in luxurious appointments.

Before the game, Rupp gave his boys a pep talk. It must have been a sizzler. The instant it was over they rushed out of the dressing room with fire and determination in their eyes, leaving Adolph to follow. But the last man out slammed the steel door behind him and the startled Mr. Rupp discovered himself imprisoned in the dressing room. He paced the floor for most of the first half until the trainer came to his rescue. No harm was done, either.

Basketball Will Boom

The most significant statement this son of Old Kaintuck had to offer in the course of a conversation was this: "After the last war," he said, "most of the football stadia were built. All of those plants are permanent and complete. But after this war you're going to find a tremendous building boom in basketball arenas.

"At Kentucky we've already purchased four square blocks of property across from our football stadium and we're going to have a place seating 18,000 persons. You're going to find other universities doing the same thing, too. They all need it. In the post-war era, basketball will have the biggest boom of any sport in the world."

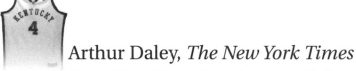

Arthur Daley, *The New York Times*

FROM OLD KAINTUCK

*Here is another colorful entry from Mr. Daley on the topic of Coach Rupp.
The Baron was an obvious favorite of Daley's, who seemed to write
about the UK coach whenever the Wildcats journeyed to Manhattan.
This article appeared in December 1948, while Kentucky was in the
process of winning its second-consecutive national title.*

That unreconstructed rebel from Old Kaintuck, Adolph Rupp, will
bring his University of Kentucky basketball team into the Garden
tomorrow, but it can't be the climactic high spot for him that it always
was in the past. Mr. Rupp has been spoiled. Last summer his dribble
heroes combined with the Phillips Oilers to win the Olympic court title
and thereby gained a half share in the championship of the world.

The Man in the Brown Suit has had his extremely talented per-
formers operating for so long that basketball fans are beginning to
wonder whether they ever graduate anybody down in Lexington. They
do, though. Kenny Rollins was handed his sheepskin last June, but he's
the only important figure on the Wildcat squad to be missing from the
roster. The rest of them began to star as freshmen and that's why
Messrs. Ralph Beard, Alex Groza, Wah Wah Jones, et al., have lingered
on the premises for such a lengthy stretch.

They probably are all infinitely better players now than they were
last season because the Olympic trip was bound to add polish to their
play. They scrimmaged constantly against the Oilers and even faced
them in a series of fund-raising games in this country before going
overseas. One of those contests produced as fantastic an ending as
basketball ever has had.

Double Jeopardy
All of the Oiler-Kentucky engagements were thriller-dillers between
the two best teams in the world. But they staged one in Kansas City
that must have been borrowed from Believe-It-Or-Not Ripley. When
the gun boomed at the end of the regulation fray, they were tied at
61–all. So they went into overtime and then into a second overtime.

The clock was running out fast as the Oilers edged ahead by a
point, 69–68. Thereupon someone in the stands touched a match to a

firecracker. It sounded just like the explosion of the timer's gun and play came to a halt. The two teams began to file off the floor. One Kentuckian took a careless, playful shot at the basket and didn't even bother to look to see whether it dropped through the hoop. But it did. Boom! The timer's gun went off to signal the actual ending of the game. Thus did the Wildcats triumph, 70–69.

Full Acceptance

The suave Mr. Rupp—also known as Old Rupp and Ready—accepted the victory with his usual aplomb. He's a courtly, colorful gent with such a rich Southern accent that one never would suspect that he originally came from Kansas. He sounds much more like the Hatfields and the McCoys. The Baron of Basketball has done some feuding up this neck of the woods, too.

The first time he brought his Kentucky team to the Garden was in 1935 when his Wildcats were beaten 23–22 by NYU, the winning point coming on the call of a foul for screening. It was then that the occasionally explosive Adolph set a new Olympic record for the running high dudgeon. He raved and he ranted at such a rank miscarriage of justice. He was still raving and ranting when he arrived home the next day to be met by newspaper men who asked him what had happened.

"I really don't know," he drawled, eyes twinkling. "But as I was driving home, I turned on the radio and got a broadcast from some church in New York. The minister used as his text: 'He was a stranger and they took him in.'" He didn't have to say another word after that. His meaning was crystal clear.

Nor is that the only occasion on which he has turned to the Bible for quotations or ideas. Just after he'd been denounced by a Big Nine coach for raiding Big Nine territory in search of players, Rupp made a speech in Ohio. He arose to his feet, cleared his throat, and said: "The subject of my talk tonight is this: A Carpetbagger in the Holy Land."

The Bigger the Better

They tell one rather apocryphal story about him that's more amusing than true. It has been said that the doorway to the Rupp office is precisely 6'2" high. He sits behind his desk and waits for basketball candidates to come through the portal for interviews.

"And if they don't bump their heads on the top of the doorway," he is supposed to have stated, "I don't even bother to shake hands."

If that were true, he wouldn't have Ralph Beard, the little gum-chewing dynamo, as the sparkplug of his team. The hustling Beard is only 5'10½", and there isn't a better basketball player in America. That's a rather strange situation for this day and age when six-and-a-half-footers are considered midgets.

But Mr. Rupp has built himself a court dynasty at Kentucky which is not unlike the football dynasty at Notre Dame. The good high school stars arrive in steady streams and Adolph has built himself pipelines to practically every high school in the state. He knows what's going on everywhere.

This Kentucky colonel is quite proud of the fact that he'd had only one dribble artist declared ineligible for failing in his studies. Those of them who take physical education have a slight advantage, it must be admitted, in the fact that the course in "Advanced Basketball" is under the direction of Professor Adolph Rupp. All his students get A marks for their efforts.

In Self-Defense

That doesn't perturb Adolph one bit. "What kind of professor gives failing grades?" he explained in self-defense. "It just proves he didn't teach his students anything." No one can question the logic of that statement.

Professor Rupp certainly knows his subject better than most, and he'd be the last to deny it. He once was detected coaching from the bench and a technical foul was called against Kentucky.

"By crimminy!" he exploded, "my coaching is worth a technical foul any time."

It probably is at that. His Wildcat squad would seem to prove it.

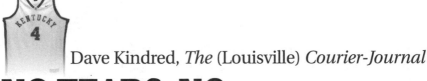

Dave Kindred, *The* (Louisville) *Courier-Journal*

NO TEARS, NO NOSTALGIA, JUST "ETERNAL THANKS" FROM ADOLPH

Dave Kindred spent the night of March 28, 1972, trying to interview Adolph Rupp following the team banquet for the Baron's final UK squad. Although it's obvious Coach Rupp wanted to continue his coaching career, he had enough respect for authority to move on.

It wouldn't be correct to say Adolph Rupp hugged the old woman. The team's banquet was over, Rupp's last as the University of Kentucky basketball coach, and he allowed himself to be hugged. The old woman went at it energetically, and Rupp looked over her shoulder, sweeping his great head to and fro. He was looking for his wife, Esther.

"Esther," the coach said, "where's Linda?" Linda is the coach's daughter-in-law. She was to leave with him.

The old woman moved away from Rupp. She shuffled sideways, and she peered back at the coach over her shoulder. Her face was aglow, and Adolph Rupp didn't notice. "Where's Linda? Get Linda, we have to leave here. Now."

It was two minutes after the banquet last night. The day before, the Kentucky brass announced that Adolph Rupp would retire. He was 70 years old. The university rules say its people retire at 70. No exceptions. So the banquet was Rupp's last, and two minutes after it was over, a television man from Lexington touched the coach's arm.

"Can we get an interview, coach?" the TV man said.

"I don't have anything to say," Rupp said. "I have to get home."

If local ties didn't work, the TV man was ready with his big stuff. "Well then, how about us doing something for CBS, coach?"

Rupp topped him. "Walter Cronkite is calling me at home tonight. That's where I'm going now." He turned away. "Linda? Where is she anyway?"

A reporter followed Rupp. Going down the long staircase outside the Grand Ballroom of the UK Student Center, the reporter moved next to the coach. "Can I ask you a couple questions on the way out?"

"Better make 'em damn quick," Rupp said. "I'm going home."

"Was there a misunderstanding between you and Dr. Singletary?" A story in the student newspaper said UK President Otis Singletary indicated there had been a misunderstanding on Rupp's retirement.

"No, not at all," Rupp said. He moved down the staircase a step at a time. He held the railing with his right hand. "We had a perfect understanding."

At the bottom of the stairs, Rupp looked back up. "Where in the hell is Linda?" He spotted his daughter-in-law. He shouted to her, "Come on, Linda, we have to go."

And Rupp walked away, moving quickly now, his head down. The reporter, trailing along at his side, said, "Then you knew this was your last year?"

Rupp threw his hands in the air, the way he might when disgruntled with a referee. "Why have I had all this harassment to go through this year?" And he walked out of the building, and he didn't look back.

What we have here is a man who has no room for sentiment. You may remark on his wit, for it is great, and you may remember his charm, for it obeys his every command even now. You may stand in awe of his personality, which is strong and overwhelms the little people and causes an old woman to hug him though he never hugs her back. But when it comes to sentiment, color him distant.

It was a perfect setting for a fond farewell, this last banquet.

The university president, Singletary, told the full house of 550 people, "There is absolutely no difference of opinion on this, the feeling of appreciation and gratitude that UK and all its friends and all basketball fans share with deep gratitude for the really wonderful, really magnificent career of the greatest coach the game of basketball has ever known."

Praise from the Governor

The governor of Kentucky, Wendell Ford, sent along a telegram saying the usual nice things, and the banquet speaker, Bill Wall, who is the outgoing president of the National Association of Basketball Coaches, said, "I know of no man in the history of basketball who has given more of himself to the game."

And yet, on this last night of a 42-year career, Adolph Rupp spoke only briefly and then said no more than protocol demanded.

Early on he said, "We should have a fine team next year. And I say 'we' because I'll be with you"—Rupp paused, and the question was palpable: would Adolph announce he'd fight the retirement and expect to win?—"in spirit." The room filled with applause.

And later he said, "To those of you who went down the glory road with me, my eternal thanks. Good night."

That was it.

No nostalgia.

No laughs.

No tears.

No sentiment.

Just good night, and where's Linda?

Gerald Eskenazi, *The New York Times*

KENTUCKY'S BARON STILL HOLDING COURT

This is a rare glimpse of Coach Rupp watching the Wildcats play in New York's 1976 NIT following his retirement. Note that in the middle of this story, he proudly tells the reporter about Lexington's new downtown arena that will be named in his honor.

He was an old man in a rumpled brown suit and a thousand people walked past him at Madison Square Garden yesterday without looking twice.

It was a return, sort of, for Adolph Rupp, but he was no longer the coach of those muscular, disciplined Kentucky basketball teams that invariably would overpower the opposition.

He was a 74-year-old former coach, who hadn't been to the Garden since 1951, before the college basketball scandals erupted. After that year, Kentucky decided to go to the National Collegiate championship instead of the National Invitation Tournament.

The Baron, as he was known, saw his teams win 879 games from 1930 until 1972, when, five years past the retirement age for most professors, he was reluctantly dropped by the school. No other coach has won as many games.

"I was never afraid of New York," he said as he waited for the start of the Kentucky-Niagara game, which opened the NIT program. "I always believed in doing things on the road just like at home. I took my boys out to see Sophie Tucker at that club—what's the name?—the Copacabana. Do they still have that place?"

Some persons, though, were afraid of the big city, Rupp recalled.

"There was that coach at Rhode Island State, Frank Keaney," he said. "You know how he would practice in his gymnasium? He'd put a smudge pot in there so his boys could get used to the smoke and smell of Madison Square Garden."

Persons who were around during the scandals have a vague recollection that Rupp gloated when some players on City College and other schools were unmasked as point-shavers. Then most of the

Kentucky starters in an NIT game held two years before—March 14, 1949—admitted having taken $1,500 apiece to fix that contest.

"People told me I should have known what was going on," said Rupp. "Hell, we won the NCAA and the NIT and we sent the team to the Olympics with those same players. If I was supposed to know what was going on when a team like that is winning, then why doesn't a coach of a losing team think his players are fixing games?"

It was the only time yesterday that Rupp raised his voice. Watching his team play Niagara, he sat quietly, almost stonily.

Once, though, he held up three fingers, inadvertently sending in a play. And a few times he applauded. Never, though, did he permit himself the beginning of a grin.

"No, I haven't been to the Garden since," he said. "But I knew my way around New York better than most people. Hell, from 1925 to 1929 I went to Columbia University. I took two advanced degrees there.

"You know next year we're opening a new building that's going to hold more people than Madison Square Garden—23,600 seats. It'll be called Rupp Arena."

Little wonder. For Rupp brought the city of Lexington, where the university is located, the national championship in 1948, 1949, 1951, and 1958. A pro franchise was created around one of his teams. His Wildcat Fives won 27 Southeastern Conference titles.

"I was the most vicious recruiter in the world," he said with irony. "Well, 87 percent of my players came from Kentucky."

Why was he so successful? "I had a different practice schedule from anyone else," he said. "My players knew exactly how long it was. When that minute hand was up, the practice was up. So they couldn't fool around. Every day—every day, you understand—we had 30 minutes of shooting drills. The first seven minutes were freelancing. Then 14 minutes in dribbling and hook shots under the baskets. Then drills for the centers and forwards, then drills for the guards."

Some of his observations, in which he rates coaches, players, and games, will go into a book.

"I rate only the players my teams went against," he said. "First, I put Jerry West. Then Tom Gola. Then Guy Rodgers. We never played Wilt or Oscar Robertson.

"The greatest coaches? I have them in no special order. They include Nat Holman, Clair Bee, Joe Lapchick, John Wooden, Hank Iba.

"The greatest games? The triple overtime with Temple in 1968, when Vernon Hatton threw from beyond the center line in second overtime at the buzzer. And then Bill Bradley, Princeton, in the NCAA semifinals in Portland. He did everything in that game that a player can do."

He noted that many of his "all-time" coaches came from New York.

"Most of them worked with Jewish ballplayers in those days," he said. "They were all very smart ball-handlers, the best I've ever seen. Now the game's complexion has changed, and I'm not talking in terms of color. I mean in style.

"We have all the smart coaches in Ohio and Indiana and Kentucky now."

Some of that dominance was evident as Rupp watched the Wildcats score a 67–61 victory, which brought Kentucky's overall Garden record to 25 victories and 10 defeats.

Word of his appearance apparently had spread. Fans of all ages walked up to him, forming a receiving line. They included 10-year-olds asking for his autograph and 30-year-olds asking if the old man remembered their cousin "from the 1946 team."

"Sure, I used to get into a lot of arguments," said the Baron. "I was blunt. But was I right? Time is the greatest proof."

Dave Kindred, *The Washington Post*

THE RIGHT MIXTURE OF LOVE, HATE KEPT RUPP ON TOP

Following Adolph Rupp's death, Dave Kindred took a look back at the Baron's career. Kindred had moved on to The Washington Post, *which moved this story on to papers across the nation.*

That curmudgeon of a coaching genius, Adolph Rupp, was 70 years old when he stopped a basketball practice at the University of Kentucky. Some poor sinner had hesitated momentarily on a layup, allowing the shot to be blocked. Before there was Wooden, before McGuire, when Smith and Knight and Crum were babes, there was Adolph Rupp. And even at 70, in his last season, the sight of a blocked layup moved him to anger, sarcasm, and inimitable theatrics.

"You get the ball like this" in the khaki shirt and trousers that was his practice uniform forever, Rupp held his hands waist high, hefting an imaginary basketball which he raised slowly overhead as he spoke again to the sinner "and then you say, 'Our Father Who art in Heaven, hallowed be Thy name, Thy kingdom come, Thy will be done, I am now going to shoot the damned basketball!'"

We hope our lives will be whole. There is a time for dying, a time when we have loved well and been loved, a day when our best work is finished. It makes sense that way, death does, and so it seemed good somehow that Adolph Rupp would die only minutes after Kentucky beat Kansas the other night. Death stole him from cancer's pain at 76, and the basketball game was undeniable evidence of the wholeness of his life.

Born of 19th-century German immigrants who wrested survival from the dust of southeast Kansas, Rupp played basketball in the early '20s at Kansas University. Kentucky hired him in 1930. In 42 seasons he won 82 percent of his games by creating teams that were models of simplicity and fire. They took hold of the ball and ran like hell. They won national championships and endured point-shaving tragedies.

Rupp's career was epic. In a poor, rural state, he created an eternal wellspring of pride, the blessed Wildcats, and Kentuckians loved him for it. In turn he gave them his life, and it was good that the latest Kentucky team, coached by one of his old players, was ranked number one in the country the night he died. It beat Kansas, 73–66.

The old man would have liked that. He had no patience with obvious namby-pambies who believed that playing well was reward in itself, that winning didn't really matter. "Why in hell do they keep score then?" Rupp said. He always worried about winning. "My stomach feels like I've swallowed a bottle of lye," he said one night before Kentucky played a patsy. "You'd think that after 40 years I'd get used to it, but I haven't." Kentucky won by 15.

His efforts to assure victory were mighty and unforgettable. "Rupp was unique," said Bill Spivey, one of his All-Americans. "He wanted everybody to hate him and he succeeded. He called us names some of us had never heard before." The resulting fear, or loathing, worked two ways. Either the player quit or he worked twice as hard. "Those that stayed wanted to show Rupp we weren't the dirty names he called us," Spivey said.

The practice floor was Rupp's stage. He once thought Bob McCowan, a guard, dribbled too much. "McCowan!" the coach thundered. Practice stopped, as if the Great Coach in the Sky had spoken. The arena was church-quiet. "McCowan, if you want to keep the ball, we'll just give you a ball to take to your room and you can sleep with it. But for now, will you by damn pass the ball?"

A center, Art Laib, timidly pursued a rebound. Rupp's Kansas-plains twang filled the air. His great fleshy ear lobes wiggled in time with his indignation. Sarcasm was the tone when Rupp said to Laib, "What's a nice Christian boy like you doing in a place like this?"

Beyond Rupp's ferocious ability to motivate players and his early realization that running was the way to win, he made basketball important not only in Kentucky but across the country by the power of his robust personality. He set records for vanity that will not soon be surpassed.

When asked in 1930 why he, a high school coach, should be hired ahead of 70 other applicants for the Kentucky job, he said, "Because I'm the best damned coach in the nation." And what was the secret to Kentucky's 1948 and '49 national championships? "That's easy," Rupp said. "It's good coaching."

Newspapermen loved him. If a reporter had nothing to write about, he could always call Rupp, who liked to see his name in print. "Why, I'd put the center jump back and take off the backboard and net.

Just leave the hoop. And raise the hoop five feet," Rupp once said to a New York writer who asked how the game could be improved. One of Rupp's players heard the outlandish suggestion and asked if Rupp meant it.

"Hell, no," Rupp said. "But anything for a column."

Rupp's appetites were large, whether the coach was hungry for attention or chili. "Gawdammit, what do you mean writing that I 'wolfed' down my chili?" he said to an offending writer. Even as he spoke, Rupp wolfed down chili, the spoon disappearing into the darkness of his throat. Working on a steak, Rupp was ruthless. He said you could sort the prospects from the suspects by watching them eat.

"Why, if a boy is aggressive with his eating, then he's going to be aggressive on the basketball floor." Rupp said, "Lordy, you should have seen Cliff Hagan!" Rupp poked at his eight-ounce filet. "See this? Hagan would have eaten this in three bites: chomp, chomp, CHOMP!"

Rupp sometimes favored a liquid diet. "I'd check the pantry to see how the bourbon was doing," he said. His last year at work, a tired old man, Rupp sat at courtside before practice. His eyes dropped shut.

"The legislature should pass a law," he said, awakening with a smile, "that at 3:00 every afternoon, any basketball coach who is 70 years old gets a shot of bourbon. These damned bouncing, bouncing, bouncing basketballs are putting me to sleep."

But he didn't want to retire. At 69, he said, "Retire? Why, what would I do? Time would hang heavy on my hands. It's the competitiveness. I like taking a bunch of boys and seeing what I can do with them. These young squirts come in as coaches at other places, and they say they're going to put an end to Rupp and Kentucky. Well, we'll see about that."

His friend Happy Chandler, the former Kentucky governor and U.S. senator, once asked him, "Why Adolph? Do you want to die on the bench?" And Rupp said, "I can't think of any place better."

Though he threatened to fight the university's mandatory retirement-at-70 rule, Rupp finally gave in. He was a wealthy man with interests in cattle, land, and tobacco. In retirement he yet appeared at coaching clinics, made speeches, and, for a while, had his own television show. He kept an office in Memorial Coliseum, the 11,500-seat gymnasium his success built, and Kentucky gave him an easy chair in the front row at the dazzling 23,000-seat palace they opened last year. Its name: Rupp Arena.

A year and a week ago, Rupp sat in the living room of his home. Silver trophies given to him in recognition of his coaching genius were scattered around the room. "I've got 40 more under my bed," he said. A tiny chair near the fireplace, left there for the happy times when his grandson visited, held a plaque certifying Rupp's induction into basketball's Hall of Fame.

Rupp talked for an hour. As he could be cantankerous, so could he be charming. He said he once stopped along a back road to buy a country ham and gave the store owner a check. "I signed it in big letters, Adolph F. Rupp, and said proudly to the owner, 'Do you know who that is?' The old guy looked at the check and looked at me and said, 'Well, sir, I'm a-hoping it's you.'"

The cancer was in Rupp then and he said so, but he asked that it not be written in the newspaper. "Just say I'm awful weak," he said. His voice, once thunder, was a whisper. "I'm as happy as I'll ever be. And I'm not a bit bitter about anything."

Walking his guest to the door, Rupp moved slowly, limping a bit. He'd had three operations in three years. It was a cold day and snow covered Rupp's yard. "It's been one of the worst winters I can remember," Rupp said. "I'm looking forward to the spring."

IN SHADOWS, HE WORKED BESIDE RUPP

The man next to Adolph Rupp throughout the Baron's career was Harry Lancaster. He was UK's top assistant coach until 1968, when he was promoted to athletics director, a position he held until 1975. Billy Reed remembered Lancaster following his death in February 1985.

Back in 1968, when I was on the University of Kentucky beat for *The Courier-Journal*, Adolph Rupp came down with a serious case of the flu before an important televised game against Vanderbilt.

All week, Harry Lancaster, his longtime assistant, had run the practices and prepared the team. Yet, come time for the game, here was Rupp in his trademark brown suit, so feeble that he barely could wave when the UK students chanted "Hello, Adolph!"

After UK's 85–80 victory, Rupp immediately returned to his sick bed, leaving Lancaster to handle his newspaper interviews and his radio show with Cawood Ledford.

"He had no business being here," said Lancaster, smiling, "but I think he wanted to protect me in case we lost."

That was Harry for you.

I remembered that game yesterday in the wake of Lancaster's death because it seemed rather typical of the 22 years that Harry spent at Rupp's side and in The Baron's massive shadow.

As almost every one of Rupp's former players will tell you, Lancaster always did a lot more coaching than Rupp ever gave him credit for.

But Harry's ego was such that he was able to understand, and accept, that the only way to get along with Rupp was to work quietly, in the background, while The Baron took the bows.

The death of Lancaster, after a long and painful bout with cancer, naturally saddened everyone who had known him, loved him, and been around him.

Yet, as former UK player John Brewer (class of '57) also pointed out, "It was a blessing." In the last year or so, as his health degenerated,

Lancaster was only a shadow of the robust man who inspired almost as much fear as Rupp and maybe even more respect.

"He was," said Brewer, "one of the toughest, but fairest, guys I've ever known. I called him about 10 days ago and told him, 'Coach, I got a lot more out of you than you got out of me.' He was kind of a Bobby Knight ahead of his time."

For me, it always has been difficult to square my experiences with Lancaster with the image portrayed by former UK players from the 1940s and '50s.

Of course, I got to know Harry well in the mid-1960s, when he probably had mellowed a bit. I always found him friendly, warm, and interesting. He loved to play golf and have a good time and he was the world's greatest at telling Rupp stories.

Fortunately, he put a lot of those stories in a book he did a few years ago in cooperation with Ledford. He didn't pull any punches, as the following anecdote indicates:

After the Southeastern Conference tournament finals in Louisville one night, my phone rang with the warning, "You'd better get up here. Coach Rupp is into an argument with the sportswriter from Knoxville and I'm afraid there's going to be trouble."

I hurried up to Adolph's room just in time to see this fellow sort of pushing Rupp around. I went over and got between them, but when this fellow persisted, I hit him.

He had been standing right in front of the bathroom and he fell over into the tub, which was full of iced-down beer. He looked so peaceful just sitting there on top of that ice and beer.

Lancaster never became a head coach, because every time he would get a decent offer, Rupp would begin making noises about retiring, which would make Lancaster decide to stick around.

Finally, instead of succeeding Rupp, Lancaster became his boss after Bernie Shively, UK's athletics director since 1938, died of a heart attack in 1968.

After a protracted search, the university tapped Lancaster to be Shively's successor, opening the way for Joe B. Hall to move up from number two assistant and become Rupp's heir apparent.

When Lancaster moved up, he and Rupp moved apart. As Rupp told it, Lancaster called him into his office and said, vindictively, "Now I'm your boss."

Harry's version differed, of course, but it's a fact that Lancaster didn't support Rupp in 1972 when The Baron tried to force UK to make an exception for him when he reached the university's mandatory retirement age of 70.

For the next several years, Rupp bore a grudge against Lancaster, Hall, and Dr. Otis Singletary, the UK president. However, when Rupp went into the hospital for the last time in 1977, Lancaster visited him and made amends.

Dan Issel, UK's all-time scoring leader who's now winding up a historic career in the National Basketball Association, was a Rupp supporter who also understood Lancaster's position.

"I think Coach Rupp thought that because Harry had been his assistant all those years, he could do anything he wanted," Issel said yesterday by phone from Phoenix, Arizona. "But Coach Lancaster had to be responsible to everyone else in the athletic department. He told coach Rupp 'no' a few times and coach Rupp didn't like it."

But as coaches, Rupp and Lancaster were the best in the business from 1946 through '68. Both wore starched khaki shirts and trousers to UK practices, which always were conducted in tomb-like silence broken only by the squeaking of sneakers, the dribbling of balls, and their often sarcastic barks.

Their first of four NCAA championships came in the 1947–48 season with the team known as "The Fabulous Five." However, as team member Dale Barnstable related yesterday, that team might have come unraveled had it not been for Lancaster.

"We had just played Creighton and beaten them badly [65–23]," Barnstable said. "However, Coach Rupp had been on us all night. Nothing we did seemed to please him.

"On the bus home that night, a bunch of us talked about quitting. We were just fed up with the criticism and the sarcasm. However, Coach Lancaster recommended that we cool off and get together to talk about it later. He orchestrated the whole thing.

"When we got back to Lexington, we met in somebody's room— I think it was Kenny Rollins's—and we decided that, no matter what he said the rest of the season, we weren't going to let it have any effect on us."

And, of course, it didn't.

That team had a 36–3 record. And after winning the NCAA championship, the "Fabulous Five" also made up the heart of the U.S. Olympic team that won the 1948 gold medal in London.

Rupp was an assistant coach on the Olympic team. Typically Lancaster stayed home.

"What's sad," Barnstable said, "is that the era of coaches who made Kentucky great—Rupp, Lancaster, Shively—now is over."

Lancaster always was able to bridge the gap between Rupp and the players. Ed Beck, starting center on the "Fiddlin' Five" NCAA title team of 1958, always will remember the compassion that Lancaster showed him when his wife, Billie, was dying of cancer in 1957.

"I think both he and coach Rupp enjoyed their reputation as tough guys," Issel said, "but both also were very kind people when you got to know them."

Lancaster served as athletics director until 1975, then turned over the job to his hand-picked successor, Cliff Hagan, the Owensboro native and Lancaster favorite who teamed with Frank Ramsey to lead the Wildcats to a 25–0 record in 1953–54.

From his retirement until the onset of his illness, Lancaster enjoyed life to the hilt despite the fact that one of his legs had to be amputated from the knee down.

He played golf at every opportunity. He loved tailgating at UK football games with his second wife, Monie, and friends. And he seemed to revel in the recognition that had come his way because of his years under Rupp and his accomplishments as athletics director.

The last time I saw Harry Lancaster laugh came before a UK football game last fall, when he had finished telling yet another Rupp story. That's how I'll always remember him.

But I guess you had to be a former player to really appreciate the man in khaki who was drill sergeant, father confessor, friend, and confidant to all those kids who took Adolph Rupp and UK basketball down the glory road.

Michael Wilbon, *The Washington Post*

HALL'S LIGHT TOUCH GIVES KENTUCKY OLD FEELING

Like many who follow in the footsteps of a legend, Joe B. Hall struggled to gain acceptance as Adolph Rupp's successor. By 1984, however, after winning a national title in 1978 and leading UK to three Final Four berths, he had settled in and began receiving his due as a coach, as is evidenced in this piece by Michael Wilbon.

Few believed the rumor that Coach Joe B. Hall had lightened his touch, that he actually cracked a few one-liners in the Kentucky locker room, and that his new approach had made the Wildcats so much more relaxed that they just might not collapse this year from the annual case of postseason anxiety.

It's no longer a rumor. Kentucky is in the Final Four, and almost every one of his players will say Hall's change in personality this year, especially his improved way of dealing with pressure, is as responsible for the team's tournament success as anything done on the basketball court.

"He's still under a lot of tension, just as he's always been," senior Sam Bowie said. "But this year he's never put a bit of it on us. And it's been extremely beneficial to a lot of us."

Hall, in his 12th year as Kentucky's head coach, has been described as "tight" and "stuffy" the past decade. He succeeded Adolph Rupp, the legend, and has never satisfied many of the people here in the bluegrass, despite having averaged nearly 23 victories a year and winning the NCAA title in 1978.

Last Saturday, after Kentucky improved to 29–4 by beating Illinois in the Mideast Regional final, Hall received what was said to be his first standing ovation in Rupp Arena.

Hall has come out of his defensive crouch, not only in public, where he has become witty and absolutely engaging, but with his players. They appreciate the change.

"Coach Hall definitely is more relaxed than in the first three years I was here," said redshirt junior Bret Bearup. "In the game, he's the same old Coach Hall, screaming up and down the court, rolling up his program and throwing it on the floor.

"But off the court, he's been able to humor the team. He comes in and jokes in the locker room. In past years after a victory, he'd come in with a look of relief, as if to say, 'I got through one more battle.'

"But this year, it looks like he's been a little more confident, at least confident enough to know the team can handle situations. I think Coach Hall is just getting better with age. When pressure needs to be exerted, he exerts it. But he's really treated us like a mature team, and I think it helps us play better."

Hall agrees. "It is a little easier this year," he said Tuesday afternoon, "because we have so many seniors. We have five, and two are fifth-year players.

"That gives us a mature team and allows the team to develop its own tempo, on and off the court. It makes it easier for the coaches. And yes, I have used a softer touch this year."

Dicky Beal, the senior point guard, agrees having so many experienced players is an advantage. "Coach Hall only has to tell us one time," he said. "We understand. And he's helped us understand the pressure of playing basketball and being in the program.

"Before this year, we took it all wrong, wanting to win for the fans and all the pressure that comes with that. You can't approach it that way. Coach Hall still drives us; that's the kind of man he is and that's his style. But we know we have to do it for the team. Everybody has been much more relaxed."

Some observers believe that the basketball supporters at Kentucky, some of them in the athletic department, have long wanted Hall to lighten up, change his image and be more accessible to the public and media.

After all, Kentucky had been ranked near the top of the polls in each of the past four seasons, with some very talented players, but was unable to make it to the Final Four.

The change, perhaps, had to come this year. But whether it was a public relations move, something to help the team through the enormous expectations, or even a conscious decision is difficult to tell.

Will Hall be able to relax as much next year when he has to replace seniors Bowie, Melvin Turpin, Jim Master, Beal, and reserve forward Tom Heitz?

Hall has even been able to joke about that eventuality recently. "Maybe I'll just go out and get some 5'8" guys and become coach of the year."

At the same press conference, Hall joked about his team's regular-season game against Illinois, when a snowstorm prevented the officials from getting to the game in Champaign, Illinois. A college professor and a high school basketball coach were two of the replacements.

"I'd be glad to have those guys again," Hall said. "It was the first time I ever had an official actually come over to me after the game and ask for an autograph."

D.G. FitzMaurice, *Lexington Herald-Leader*

HALL'S A COMPLEX MAN WHO UPHELD TRADITION

Lexington Herald-Leader *columnist D.G. FitzMaurice provides an interesting retrospective on the career of Joe B. Hall following Hall's 1985 retirement.*

"My friends tell me you're trying to get me out of coaching."
  "Then get new friends."

"We've been through quite a few media days together, haven't we?"
  "Yes, we have."
  "Let's both have good years."

Those two conversations, one intimidating, the other intimate, took place many seasons apart, yet both involved Kentucky coach Joe Hall and a member of the media. In a way they reflect the complex nature of the man who just announced his retirement from the most pressurized position in college basketball.

The first incident occurred in the summer of 1973, before Hall's second season at Kentucky. He had failed in his quest to land any of the nation's three top big men—Kent Benson, Tommy LaGarde, and Tree Rollins—and in an effort to be facetious, I had written something to the effect that had Hall been a member of the Royal Canadian Mounted Police, he would have been drummed out of the corps because he didn't get his man.

Hall, outraged at the article, stormed into the sports department where we settled the issue like any other two grown-up people—we shouted at each other for a good, or rather, bad 45 minutes.

The Kentucky coach had erroneously interpreted my remark, "drummed out of the corps," as my way of saying he should be fired. Thus the reference to friends and new friends.

The second conversation took place before last season at the school's annual preseason media day activities.

Hall, sitting on a table, surveyed the scene of eager, young reporters before motioning me, an old face in the crowd, to join him.

That's when, in especially warm fashion, he referred to our relationship, which went back to the days when he was Adolph Rupp's top assistant.

Both episodes, I think, reveal various facets of Joe Hall's personality.

By turns, Hall could be compassionate or cold, charming or distant, understanding or intransigent, humorous or humorless, intimidating or insecure, sometimes all in the same day.

But beneath it all, buried under all the layers we mortals habitually envelop ourselves in, a simple fact emerges—Joe Hall is a good human being who helped keep the Kentucky tradition alive.

As I skim over recent UK basketball history, I am more and more convinced that Hall was the only man who could have successfully succeeded Rupp at Kentucky in 1972.

As a youngster growing up in Cynthiana, Kentucky, Hall became easily enamored with Kentucky basketball. After graduating from high school, he played for Rupp and then became Rupp's number one assistant.

Hall, then, by both temperament and experience, appeared to be uniquely qualified to succeed Rupp, the winningest basketball coach in college history.

But it wasn't easy.

Pressures fairly permeated Hall's office at Memorial Coliseum. There was the pressure of following a legend, the pressure of the Kentucky program itself, the pressure, real or imagined, from a liberated local media, and, perhaps, some self-inflicted pressures as well.

Certainly, the acrimony following Rupp's forced retirement did little to ease Hall's transition from assistant to head coach.

Rupp, who had openly endorsed another UK assistant, Gale Catlett, as his successor, retained an office in Memorial Coliseum after his retirement, and there were those who thought Rupp was guilty of exerting extra pressure on Hall by continuing to appear on his weekly television show after Hall had become head coach and had a television show of his own.

"When I first took the job," Hall said yesterday, "I sensed an attitude of respect for Rupp, and there were those who almost hoped I wouldn't make it."

No doubt Hall very quickly realized he was not immune to the pressure of a program that is larger than any single individual, and a 13–13 season his second year did little to ease tension.

Concurrent with these happenings, a more subtle change was occurring in local sports reporting.

A new breed of sportswriters, no longer content at being considered a mere extension of the school's sports information department, began assuming a more independent stance. Adversary relationships became virtually inevitable on occasion, and Hall, who had witnessed the media's cozy relationship with Rupp, fumed with frustration.

Hall, who never mastered the art of orchestrating a segment of a willing press, also encountered difficulties with a portion of the national media.

Hall, however, was justified in many of his complaints, for there were those reporters who engaged in "instant history" reporting during UK's march to the 1978 NCAA national championship. The Wildcats were the bad guys while the Duke Blue Devils wore the white hats. It was nonsense, of course, but Hall is still plagued by questions concerning the gravity of the Kentucky program.

Throughout his 13-year tenure at Kentucky, both Hall and the press have been occasionally guilty of insensitivity, neither party, perhaps, appreciating the role of the other.

"I hold no malice towards the press," said Hall yesterday. "Looking back, I can see the media's position on just about everything. I think I respect what your job is now that I'm out of coaching, and I hope you respect what I did to protect the program."

The Program. Always The Program.

Hall will be remembered for his stewardship of the Kentucky program. As Athletics Director Cliff Hagan noted on Friday, Hall has not only carried on the Kentucky tradition, he has enhanced it.

For it was Hall who really broke the color line at Kentucky, and it was Hall who kept the faith by continuing the standard of excellence that has become synonymous with Kentucky basketball.

Not bad for a little old country boy from Cynthiana.

Scott Fowler, *The Washington Post*

COUNTED DOWN AND OUT, KENTUCKY INJECTED WITH NEW LIFE BY PITINO

*For Kentucky, Rick Pitino was the right person at the right time, inject-
ing the program with energy and pride that resulted in three Final Four
berths and the 1996 national championship. His first Wildcat team in
1990 was such a departure from the previous year's squad that had lost
19 games that national media outlets, such as* The Washington Post,
immediately began to notice the changes in Lexington.

Twelve thousand people, many of them waving huge numeral threes
and wearing "Pitino's Bombinos" sweatshirts, spread out over half-
empty Rupp Arena a couple of Thursday nights ago.

The crowd was about the size that preseason doomsayers had predicted for the University of Kentucky's next-to-last home game. By that
time, they figured, the magic wand Rick Pitino supposedly wielded
would have turned to dust. The Wildcats would be something like
5–20, and everyone associated with the school's first year of a three-
year NCAA probation would be properly humiliated.

That October theory has run into two major problems in February.
For one, Kentucky is 14–12 and needed only to defeat Auburn at home
last Saturday to sail through Southeastern Conference play with a 9–0
home record, which it did with a 98–95 victory over the Tigers. After
contending strongly for the league title, Kentucky (10–7 in the conference) should end up no worse than fourth.

The other snag: the 12,000 Kentucky fans were waiting patiently to
hear Pitino's postgame radio show, which is piped over Rupp Arena
loudspeakers. They represented about half of the Rupp's record crowd
of 24,311, which witnessed the Wildcats' unlikely 100–95 victory over
then ninth-ranked Louisiana State University.

Pitino, nearing the end of his first season as the ringleader of the circus known as Kentucky basketball, still isn't quite used to the adulation.

"This," he said, sweeping one arm toward the fans, "is remarkable."

It has been a rather remarkable season for Kentucky, and not solely in terms of wins. There was a time not long ago when a coach who could barely boost the Wildcats above .500 would have provoked the same response as a $100 losing ticket at the Kentucky Derby.

But that was before April 1988, when an Emery Air Freight envelope addressed to a Kentucky recruit's father popped open in Los Angeles and $1,000 in $50 bills spilled out. Former assistant coach Dwane Casey still insists that the envelope he sent to Claud Mills contained only a basketball game videotape and now has a multimillion dollar lawsuit pending against Emery.

The NCAA didn't agree. After a probe of the Kentucky basketball office, it nearly shut the program down for a season. Instead, the Wildcats were banned from postseason tournaments this season and in 1991, banned from live television games this season, and had their basketball scholarships reduced. (The third year of Kentucky's NCAA term is probationary, without sanctions.)

Kentucky played the 1988–89 season shadowed by the NCAA and finished 13–19, the school's first losing season in 62 years. The entire coaching staff was forced out. Three starters left the squad because of the probation, and the NCAA would not permit Kentucky to replace those players' scholarships.

Thus the predictions of doom. The SEC media picked Kentucky to finish ninth in the 10-team conference, ahead of only Auburn. One national magazine forecast the Wildcats would go 1–17 in the SEC.

But Pitino, whom Kentucky athletics director C.M. Newton had lured away from the NBA's New York Knicks after Eddie Sutton resigned, *talked privately* even in the preseason about winning the SEC. He motivated his players with early morning workouts and promises of a new, up-tempo style.

"We'd be struggling out to a 5:00 AM practice, and Coach Pitino would be yelling, 'Get up! Get up! LSU's not practicing now, they're still in dreamland!'" Kentucky point guard Sean Woods said, "Guys would be looking at each other saying, 'This guy is crazy.'"

The rigorous practices have enabled Pitino to employ a seven-man rotation and still press for most of every game. Pitino did not inherit a single player above 6'7", making this the shortest Kentucky team since the 1962–63 season, when Lexington Mayor Scotty Baesler was still suiting up for the Wildcats. But he did happen upon a squadron of excellent three-point shooters and quick learners.

Derrick Miller, the team's only senior, scores more than half of his 19 points a game from beyond the three-point stripe. Reggie Hanson,

Kentucky's center and another accomplished outside shooter (16 points per game), effectively unclogs the lane by forcing opponents such as LSU's 7'1" Shaquille O'Neal to guard him on the perimeter. Forwards Deron Feldhaus and John Pelphrey, along with reserves Jeff Brassow and Richie Farmer, each average at least one three-pointer per game.

Kentucky set five national three-point records in a six-game stretch in December, once attempting 53 three-pointers in a 116–113 overtime loss to Southwestern Louisiana. It still leads the country in successful three-point shots per game, at 10.5.

But since SEC play began and teams have defended more aggressively against Kentucky's three-pointers, the smaller Kentucky players frequently have been able to sneak in for backdoor layups.

"I'd put the 'three' only fourth or fifth on the reasons for our success now," Pitino said. "Number 1 is our press, and number 1A is our motion offense that we've been getting so much out of."

Kentucky's press either befuddles the opposition or invites it to hold a slam-dunk contest. Kansas dissected Kentucky with its crisp passing by an astounding 150–95 margin in December. But, except for that debacle, Kentucky has played well above expectations. Even its own.

"I'll be very honest. There's no way I expected this," said Feldhaus, a bruising sophomore forward whose father, Allen, played under Adolph Rupp from 1960 to 1962. "Before Coach Pitino came, I didn't think there would be any way we would be a factor in the SEC race."

The Wildcats have upset the team then atop the SEC on four occasions this season. If not for its consistently lackluster performances away from Lexington, Kentucky's 12–2 overall record in Rupp Arena could have provided the foundation for an 18- to 20-win season. Kentucky's scrappy, pressing attack probably has contributed to the three scuffles in which the Wildcats have been involved this season, most recently when Hanson and Alabama's Robert Horry mixed it up February 17 and were ejected. Pitino and LSU Coach Dale Brown also had a well-publicized shouting match in January.

The boldness is no surprise, however, given that Pitino has instructed his team to become "extensions of my personality" on the court. Pitino's sideline show itself often is worth the price of admission, as he thrashes about in his $700 Armani suits, occasionally hyperventilates, and takes pride in never sitting down.

"Do you realize the guy never sits down?" Miller asked. "That's what's incredible."

With three blue-chip recruits coming in and only Miller leaving, the Wildcats appear in a strong position to challenge for the SEC title again. But now that the basketball community has been caught off guard once by a better-than-usual Kentucky team, it's doubtful that will happen again.

"We've all had a good part in bringing Kentucky basketball back," said Miller, who will play his final game for Kentucky on the road against Notre Dame March 5. "We'll finish off strong this season, and the expectations will be high again, just like they always were."

Timothy W. Smith, *The New York Times*

AT KENTUCKY, TRADITION TAKES A TWIST

Tubby Smith was the obvious choice to take over at Kentucky in May 1997. Because of the prominence of the position, his hiring was seen by many, including The New York Times, *as evidence that the South had made huge strides on the matter of race.*

One of the first things that Tubby Smith did after being named Kentucky's head basketball coach last May was to visit Adolph "Herky" Rupp Jr., the son of the legendary Wildcats coach.

Smith wanted to make a connection to the past, wanted Coach Rupp's son to know that the Wildcats' winning tradition was safe in his hands. But like everyone else, Smith wanted to know what Adolph Rupp would have thought about the hiring of the first black head coach of the school's celebrated men's basketball team.

"If my father were alive today, he would welcome Tubby Smith with open arms and congratulate him on getting the job," Herky Rupp said in a recent phone conversation. "And as a former coach, my father would do anything he could to help him. There is a popular misconception that my father was a racist. It's just not true. When he was coaching high school in Freeport, Illinois, back in 1927, my father had a black kid on his basketball team."

But the issue is not what Rupp might think. It is what the basketball world, including C.M. Newton, Kentucky's director of athletics, and many of his colleagues know as fact: talent and acumen are colorless. Witness Orlando "Tubby" Smith.

In his six-year head-coaching career at Tulsa (1991–95) and Georgia (1995–97), Smith compiled a record of 124–62 (66.7 winning percentage), including a 45–19 record (70.3) at Georgia. His teams have been to the National Collegiate Athletic Association tournament four straight years, and he has taken three to the Round of 16.

However, it is hard to escape the twist of his latest job. Smith is now the head coach at the university that represented the racial segregation of college basketball when the 1966 national championship game pitted Kentucky's all-white team (Rupp's Runts) against Don Haskins's Texas Western squad, which had five black starters.

"They played that game at Cole Field House at Maryland, and I remember as a kid rooting for Texas Western against Kentucky," said Smith, who grew up in Scotland, Maryland. "I was rooting to bring down barriers, but more so because it was people of color, black people, participating in the NCAA tournament and winning. It gave us all a dream and a hope that we could get to this point."

In case anyone thinks that Smith, 46, is some kind of overnight sensation, he reminds you that he has been at this for 23 years—including 12 as a college assistant and the last six as a head coach. He had a previous stop at Kentucky, spending two seasons as an assistant under Rick Pitino, who left the Wildcats to coach the Boston Celtics in the National Basketball Association, opening the way for Smith.

"Tubby Smith was the only person on the list," Newton said of the candidates to replace Pitino. "He was a no-brainer. If he had turned down the job, then I would have had to make a list. He had a great track record; he had connections to Kentucky and familiarity with the program and the way we do things here."

Newton, 67, was a pioneer in the integration of Southern college sports nearly three decades ago. As Alabama's basketball coach, he bucked the system—and the legendary football coach Paul "Bear" Bryant—and gave a basketball scholarship to a black player named Wendell Hudson. Newton understood the hoopla then, but he doesn't understand what the big deal is with Smith's being named the Kentucky coach.

Smith is not the first black head coach at Kentucky. Bernadette Mattox, who had also been part of Pitino's staff, has that distinction after being hired as the women's basketball coach in 1995. However, the men's team is as revered as a state treasure.

"It's really bothersome, because I thought we were past all that," Newton said. "This is different. This is a different era."

Smith hasn't forgotten what the past was like.

"I remember growing up in segregated southern Maryland," said Smith, the sixth-youngest of 17 children who grew up on a farm. "There were few black people in the area we grew up in. But we were accepted by people because my dad was a hard-working guy. People respected that about him. What I've tried to do over the years is work hard and try to let my accomplishments represent who I am."

When integration came, the all-black George Washington Carver School was closed and the students were moved to all-white Great

Mills High School. Smith joined the integrated student committee "to help keep racial harmony."

"There were kids wanting to fight every day," he said. "Kids were mad because they closed down their schools and put them in a different environment."

Soon the white students stopped seeing Tubby Smith, the black student, and began seeing Tubby Smith, the peacemaker and all-state track athlete and basketball team captain.

He attended High Point College in North Carolina on an athletic scholarship and by his count was one of only three black students on campus. And though it was a time of racial tension, Smith was appointed co-captain of the basketball team as a junior and the team captain as a senior.

"Because of the things in my background, I think I was a little more equipped to handle the jobs at the University of Georgia and the University of Kentucky," he said.

That ability to size up a situation in the blink of an eye, to take problems and turn them upside down and inside out and come up with solutions has helped make Smith a successful basketball coach. He is a superb defensive strategist, a great recruiter, and an excellent motivator.

Smith is taking over a team that won the national championship two years ago and lost in the title game last season. Even though he doesn't have Ron Mercer and Derek Anderson—who have departed for the National Basketball Association—he has enough talent to be competitive in the Southeastern Conference. He certainly has more talent than he did when he took over at Georgia in 1995. That team, which included his son G.G. at point guard, went 21–10 and lost to Syracuse in the Round of 16. G.G. remained at Georgia for his junior year, but Smith's 18-year-old son Saul will play guard at Kentucky, which will play the Australian national team tonight in its final exhibition before opening the season against Morehead State on Thursday.

Smith knows the pressure is on to build on what Pitino re-established at Kentucky.

"After taking the team through probation, people appreciated how hard Rick worked to restore the integrity and the winning tradition," Smith said. "He brought the glamour back. He brought that up-tempo, pressing style, with the in-your-face defense that was entertaining to watch. That's tough to replace."

The Kentucky players believe the transition will be smooth.

"As far as the type of game we'll play, there won't be much difference," said Cameron Mills, a senior guard who played on the Wildcats' 1996 championship team and whose father played for Rupp. "But the coaching styles are different, because they're two different individuals. They have a different philosophy. Coach Smith has already changed some of the team rules. With Coach Pitino, we never had a curfew. Coach Smith is giving us a curfew of midnight. He wants us to get our rest and to study.

"Not that Coach Pitino wasn't, but Coach Smith is very concerned with our academic progress. He's already made it a goal that we raise our team grade point average. He wants to make sure that we're attending all our classes and making all our study halls and our tutoring sessions."

Mills said he recently walked past the open door of Smith's office, and the coach invited him to come in and sit down and chat "about nothing really—classes, sports, life."

George Felton, who hired Smith as an assistant when he was head coach at South Carolina but is now Smith's assistant at Kentucky, admires that part of the new coach's personality. "His ability to relate to people from all walks of life has helped him tremendously on the college level," Felton said. "The great thing about Tubby is if you don't know him and you sit down with him, afterward you'll feel like you've known him for 10 years."

It didn't take long for Herky Rupp to warm up to the latest of his father's successors.

"Coach Smith fits the mold of a Kentucky coach," Rupp said. "He's down home, down to earth, not aloof, not flaunting his position. My father was the same way. You'd find my father at his grandson's little league game, or at a cattle show or at Brookings Restaurant eating chili. He was a part of the community because he wanted to be, not because it was part of some promotion.

"Coach Smith is the same way. He's not just passing through. He wants to be here, be the Kentucky coach. He's the type of person you might run into down at the corner store, eating crackers and Vienna sausages. I'm not knocking Rick Pitino, because I've never met him and I don't know him, but it's going to be easier for the Kentucky fans to relate to Tubby Smith than to Rick Pitino."

William C. Rhoden, *The New York Times*

KENTUCKY'S NEWTON HAS COME FULL CIRCLE

As Kentucky's athletics director, C.M. Newton hired two head coaches who won national titles (Rick Pitino and Tubby Smith). But his place in history may be as the man who started five African Americans as head coach at Alabama, then later hired the first black head coach at Kentucky. The New York Times *ran this feature on Newton prior to the 1998 Final Four in San Antonio.*

As the Kentucky Wildcats took the Alamodome floor on Friday for the final practice before their Final Four game against Stanford, C. M. Newton sat courtside and took in the atmosphere. Tubby Smith, the Wildcats' first-year head coach, came over and shook his hand. Newton, Kentucky's athletics director, wished Smith luck and blessings. A day later, an overtime victory over tall, tough Stanford completed Kentucky's improbable run to the national championship game.

This was Kentucky's third straight Final Four appearance. But for the 66-year-old Newton, the journey was especially sweet after last night's one-point victory. At a news conference in Lexington last spring, Newton introduced Smith as the Wildcats' head coach. Now on this warm Texas afternoon, 34 victories later, Kentucky was pursuing its seventh national championship and second under Newton. In an uncomfortable way, this ride had stirred memories for Newton of his days as Alabama's basketball coach in the 1970's. Smith is the first African American head basketball coach at Kentucky, a milestone some thought would never happen.

There was grousing, mostly in the media, when Smith was hired. Was Smith "experienced" enough? Could he manage "off the court?" How would he relate to boosters, fans? One of the strongest reactions came from an African American columnist with the *Lexington Herald-Leader*, Merlene Davis, who advised Smith in an open letter to turn the job down because it was a no-win situation. On Friday, Davis, unswayed by this fabulous season, said that if Kentucky began to lose, the criticism aimed at Smith would be far greater because of his race. Newton said pressure on the Kentucky coach was race-blind. "If a coach loses at Kentucky, I don't care if they're green or purple, they're going to be under pressure," Newton said. "I suppose the thing that annoys me about this is that in 1998, I thought we've moved beyond that."

For Newton, all of this represented a career come full circle. His first head coaching job was in Lexington in 1956 at Transylvania College, where he integrated the program. He was hired as head coach at Alabama over the objection of some who wanted a more prominent name. His first act was to integrate that program.

Neither of Newton's major influences were integrationist. In fact, quite the opposite. His two major mentors—the Kentucky basketball coach Adolph Rupp and the Alabama football coach Paul "Bear" Bryant—are legendary figures. Each is closely associated with the racial evolution of big-time college athletics.

The upset loss of a Rupp-coached Kentucky basketball team to Texas Western in the 1966 national title game is generally credited with accelerating integration in the South, while the stunning 42–21 loss of a Bryant-coached Alabama football team to Southern Cal in 1970 accelerated integration at Alabama.

Newton played basketball at Kentucky under Rupp. He was hired in 1969 by Bryant to rebuild Alabama's decrepit basketball program.

"I think Coach Rupp and Coach Bryant were more alike than they were different," Newton said, referring to their outlooks on race and sports. "They were both pragmatists."

While coaching the basketball team at Alabama, Newton became the first Southeastern Conference coach to start five African American players. His teams were known for their disciplined, structured style of play. Bryant began to pick his brain about dealing with black athletes.

"The stereotype was that if you had an all-black team, they wouldn't be disciplined," Newton said. "Coach Bryant was a product of his time, he heard the stereotypes, he believed them. He asked me one day: 'How do you coach them? How do you treat them?' I said I coach them like you coach anyone else, treat them like you treat anyone else."

Newton added: "I'm still not sure that Coach Bryant would have integrated the team if USC hadn't come into Alabama and beaten us so badly. Remember after that game he said: 'We can no longer compete with the same kind of players. We have to change.'"

Thirty years later, Newton, faced with hiring a new coach, was pragmatic as well.

"It was going to be extremely difficult for someone to come in and follow Rick Pitino," he said. "Rick was a great communicator, had charisma, was a master teacher. The players liked him. They were disappointed that he left.

"What made me a Tubby Smith fan is that he showed that he could win with another coach's players. He went to Tulsa, where he won with another coach's players. He went to Georgia, where he won with another coach's players. That showed me he was a communicator. He has charisma in his own way and he was a master teacher."

Newton was amused last year by the hand-wringing over his decision to hire an African American basketball coach, though he learned a long time ago that the hysteria surrounding race is often founded on fear, myth, and ignorance. As an aspiring major league pitcher in the early 1950s, Newton had a choice of reporting to either a Yankees or a Brooklyn Dodgers minor league team. When Newton chose the Yankees, his father breathed a sigh of relief. He said he was glad his son chose the Yankees so he wouldn't have to compete against or play with black or Hispanic players.

"I never thought of my father as a racist, but he was a product of his time," Newton said. "Anyway, I reported to camp, and the first day, who sits down in the locker next to me but Nino Escalera." Escalera was black and Hispanic. Newton said he laughed to himself at the foolishness of it all. He has been laughing at bigotry ever since.

Neil Schmidt, *The* (Cincinnati) *Enquirer*

FIRM HANDS, LOVING HANDS

On numerous occasions, Tubby Smith has described himself as a teacher. In January 2005, The *(Cincinnati)* Enquirer's *Neil Schmidt penned this profile of Smith as a molder of young people.*

Lately, he has made it look easy. Tubby Smith has coached Kentucky to 69 basketball victories the past two and a half seasons, the most of any school in the nation, and been lauded for his deft handling of personnel.

To find his most telling time, though, try his toughest. Three seasons ago, with a talented Wildcat group unraveling its way to a "Team Turmoil" tag, the coach would often call his son, Saul, in the middle of the night.

Saul, enduring endless bus rides in the National Basketball Development League, would hear the hurt: "I don't know what to do with this kid."

Such talk—spoken about numerous players that season—might mimic a father's lament, for Tubby Smith is nothing if not involved in his players' lives. As his wife, Donna, once said, "He thinks that he can save every damn kid out there."

The pressures of leading college basketball's all-time winningest program—such as Sunday's showdown against the third-winningest school, Kansas—have nothing on the difficulties of molding mercurial teenagers. Yet for this coach, nurturing comes naturally.

After nearly eight years in the most scrutinized basketball post in America, Smith remains true to his roots as one of 17 children of a Maryland sharecropper, weaned on the values of hard work and responsibility. Every lesson learned then translates to basketball and to raising young men.

"It teaches you patience and obedience," Smith said of his upbringing's effect. "You can't rush Mother Nature.

"Kids, it takes awhile for them to mature, to grow. You've got to cultivate them; you've got to nourish them; you've got to weed them, because there's going to be times they're going to be growing wild.

"It's like a tomato plant: If you want them to grow up straight, you've got to put stakes in the side, tie them up against those stakes so they grow up straight and strong. And then you better put the right type of fertilizer in the ground to help them so their roots will grow strong."

So while many of his contemporaries adopt either business models or bullying tactics, Smith has his Wildcats channel the Waltons. What he cultivates is a disciplined, family environment.

"I'm not going to say other coaches don't do that," said Saul Smith, who played for his father and is now a Tennessee Tech assistant coach. "But there's a sense of loyalty he has to those players," Saul said. "He wants them to be better people first and foremost."

Said UK senior Chuck Hayes of his coach: "He's more of a father figure first, then a coach. He has a big heart. He always thinks of others before he thinks of himself."

Tending His Flock

Smith, 53, keeps a wooden shepherd's staff—a gift from former player Cameron Mills—in his office to remind him of his responsibilities. Like everything in Smith's story, it drips with symbolism.

A shepherd can use such a staff for discipline, smacking a wanderer back into the herd, or as a weapon, perhaps to fight off wolves. The crook is to help pull a sheep out of harm's way—say, if it gets a foot caught in the rocks.

"And the staff is strong enough, sturdy enough, to lean on when the shepherd gets tired," Smith said.

For years there would seem to have been few opportunities to rest easy.

He's the first African American to coach a program that once was slow to integrate its roster, a coach who has said he's aware that every day he represents "my family, my university, and my race."

He drew criticism for starting Saul for two years while UK endured three consecutive double-digit-loss seasons, the first such stretch of futility in school history. Fans lamented his deliberate style of play in contrast to the flashy Rick Pitino teams that preceded him, and many denied Smith credit for the national title he won in 1998 with Pitino's players.

Things came to a head two seasons ago when an 18-point defeat at archrival Louisville—coached by Pitino—dropped UK to 6–3. Chicken Littles were in full cluck.

The Wildcats responded by winning 63 of 70 games since and securing the top overall seed in the past two NCAA tournaments.

"If you are at Kentucky as the basketball coach and you get bogged down by those things external to your program, you could get paralyzed.

And you'd make a lot of dumb decisions," said former UK athletics director C.M. Newton, who hired Smith.

"Tubby believes in himself, and he doesn't get burdened by external pressure. He told me once, 'I'll tell you what pressure is. Pressure's being the father of 17 children, being black, in rural Maryland. My dad had pressure. I don't have any pressure.'"

Smith grew up in a cinder-block house with no indoor plumbing. As the second son of a farmer who also labored as a barber, bus driver, and construction worker, Smith learned to drive a tractor before he was nine and took over many duties of the farm—plowing the garden; picking tomatoes, cotton, and corn; stripping tobacco; hanging meat; feeding the hogs and chickens; and milking the cow.

Responsibility? If you didn't draw water, you didn't bathe, and if you didn't cut and haul the wood for the family's stove, you didn't have heat or couldn't eat.

"My sons, all they had to do was take the garbage can down to the corner," Smith said, laughing, "and that was tough enough."

An Outstretched Hand

Smith said his father preached perseverance and patience, with the philosophy, "All you have to do is last."

"If you've got a horse in foal, you've got to wait the season out before you reap the benefits," Smith said. "Then you've got a year or two before it matures. ... [With players], sometimes you can't rush them."

That brings us back to Team Turmoil. Smith declared on Media Day that season that he had never had a more talented team—an admission he later called "the biggest mistake I ever made."

That young team struggled with chemistry issues that included fights, suspensions, arrests, and curfew violations. Smith waited for players to mature who didn't.

"Tubby always thinks he can work with guys and help them," said UK radio analyst Mike Pratt, a former Wildcat. "Some of those guys (in 2001–02) took advantage of him because of that."

Smith consulted often with his son, Saul, who had played with many of the transgressors. After the season, five players either quit or were dismissed, as Smith learned to distance himself from problematic players.

"The sensitivity of coaching, and the caring part—you have to be able to step back (and) say, 'That's it, I've done all I can do for this particular situation,'" Smith said. "That's tough to do."

Still, there was room for understanding. Smith talked an embarrassed Jules Camara, who missed a season after a DUI arrest, out of transferring. He kept Gerald Fitch, who was twice suspended that season for violating team rules, knowing this was a player who had a rough upbringing and whose older brother, George, was killed in 1998.

"He was there for me through the tough times," Fitch said last year.

Fitch matured into the star of last season's team. Another Wildcat suspended during the '01–02 season, Princeton High product Erik Daniels, blossomed and now plays for the NBA's Sacramento Kings.

"You treat (players) like they're family, and nobody in their right mind would throw their family out to the wolves," Smith said. "You do whatever you have to to help them grow and become better people. That's my responsibility, my role as a teacher, as a coach, as a leader, as a human being."

Control and Compassion

At his introductory news conference at UK in 1997, Smith said, "My philosophy is based on love, family, and discipline."

He hasn't wavered from that. The man whose $2.5 million salary is reportedly the college game's highest is refreshingly old-fashioned and sincere.

Since his first head-coaching job at Tulsa in 1991, Smith has stopped to shake every hand courtside—opponents, referees, stats crew, his players—before each game, home or away. He often sends handwritten notes congratulating players he has recruited who signed with *other* schools, wishing them luck.

When a UK recruit, John Stewart, died in 1999 during his senior year of high school, Smith left the Wildcats during the NCAA tournament to mourn with the family. He continued to call the Stewarts every few months for four years, then made certain to include them and their late son as part of 2003 Senior Day ceremonies. He later awarded them the SEC championship ring Stewart would have earned.

"He's a humble man, and you know it off the top," Saul Smith said. "To be the highest-paid coach in America and you don't have an ego? That's pretty cool."

Though it pains him when a player goes astray, Tubby Smith stays the course. He speaks of tough love, and there's plenty tough: 6:00 AM practices much of the season, inflexible team rules, his demanding nature.

"Don't mistake niceness, cordiality, or humbleness for lack of competitiveness," Newton said. "I know of nobody that's any more competitive than Tubby."

Once players buy in, the trust is absolute. Critics and coaches marveled last season how Fitch kept cool when Smith didn't start him in an SEC tournament game, trying a different matchup.

"There's no democracy," UK associate head coach David Hobbs said. "It's a dictatorship. There's a point when you surrender to that and you believe. That's when you can really make strides."

Lasting Love, Success

The day before Smith was hired at UK, a black Lexington columnist pleaded in print for him to turn down the job, suggesting Wildcat fans weren't ready for a black head coach. She was wrong. Eight years later, Smith's secretary says he receives the least hate mail of any coach for whom she has worked—a list including Joe B. Hall, Eddie Sutton, and Pitino.

"There hasn't been that [racism] talk," Smith said. "Every time you lose, you're going to hear, 'He can't coach,' but that goes with the territory."

Last week Smith claimed his 200th victory at UK and perhaps by season's end could pass Pitino (219) for the number three spot in school history. He has done what his father would expect: lasted, endured.

He also has done what he expected: gotten through.

"Seeing young men, when they reach that maturation level that they've 'got it'—they've gotten better academically, socially, physically, spiritually—that's the most gratifying part," Smith said. "You can make a difference in people's lives."

A Kentucky fan cheers for the Wildcats before the start of the 1996 national title game against Syracuse in East Rutherford, New Jersey.

Section V
THE PHENOMENON

Lonnie Wheeler, *Blue Yonder*

BLEEDING UK BIG BLUE

Cincinnati Post *columnist Lonnie Wheeler spent the 1996–97 season working on a book,* Blue Yonder: Kentucky: The United State of Basketball, *chronicling Kentucky basketball. This excerpt does an excellent job of describing the depth and magnitude of love Kentuckians have for Wildcat basketball.*

Thursday was warm. Thursday was a festival. Little dome tents formed a linear settlement that stretched from both ticket windows out to the Avenue of Champions and around the corners. Their utterly contented occupants, squatters dressed in blue and white, tossed footballs, shared pizza, gathered around portable televisions, and caught naps on the Memorial Coliseum grass, right under the ample nose of Adolph Rupp's historical marker. As the October afternoon drifted amiably beyond 70 degrees, the happy campers entertained periodic visitations from the colony's original settler, a chesty middle-aged veteran and former plumber named Wally Clark, whose ancient roots traced all the way back to late summer. In 38 curious days of idle purpose, Clark had become legendary. He had waited longer than anyone for tickets to the University of Kentucky's first public basketball practice.

Clark's excess—everyone knew he could have saved himself three weeks and still been first in line—was so conspicuous that some folks could not let it go unanswered. Prankish students jumped on the roof of his Ford Fiesta camper one late night and slid down onto the hood. Others taunted him about getting a job, which Clark doesn't have because of a disability from a stroke he suffered six years ago. After five weeks of privileged parking, he had to move his camper by order of the Lexington police, who figured that the streets around the Coliseum might turn into a KOA as Big Blue Madness drew nearer. But all of that, and the boredom, was a toll that Clark would have gladly paid twice over for his Wildcats—and for his celebrity. On Thursday, Madness Eve, others in line noticed that Wally's walk had a little strut to it. He passed out UK buttons and paused, adjusting his sunglasses, for the various TV cameras that recorded his moment.

The cameras had come to the Coliseum not only for the Madness vigil, but also for the Basketball Media Day activities on the concourse. Inside, soft drinks were being served and three walls of curtains had been erected for Rick Pitino's preseason news conference. A few minutes after the appointed hour, the coach emerged through the front curtain, bouncy and dapper as usual in a striped shirt with a bright white collar and tie. Demonstrating that despite his recent fame and outrageous popularity he is still a coach first and a personality after that. Pitino went straight into his scouting report on Clemson, which, in four weeks, would be the first opponent in Kentucky's defense of its 1996 NCAA championship.

He talked on, informatively, about his new big men—he has never had genuine pivot people on the order of freshman Jamaal Magloire and little-used sophomore Nazr Mohammed in his seven previous seasons at Kentucky—and about needing three NBA draft picks these days to win an NCAA title, implying, roundabout, that Ron Mercer and Derek Anderson put his team two-thirds of the way there. "I think Ron Mercer is getting ready to bust out and have an incredible year," Pitino said, playing to the imaginations in his audience. And then somebody asked about Wally Clark.

"We've gotten to know Wally very well here. He showers and shaves here, comes in in the morning with no shirt on and has his coffee. I tell people back home [in New York] that he has camped here for 38 days, and they ask, 'Why 38 days? Couldn't he have done it with 20 days?' I say, 'Yes.' They say, 'Then why did he do it?' I say, 'I can't answer that. You'll have to ask Wally.'" Pitino then slips back through the curtain, out of sight and reach.

Wally has been asked that, of course, and his answer is specific. He was on a mission. Starting in 1989 and four times after that, a man named Robert Vallandingham was first in line, with his family, for what was then called Midnight Madness. The problem was that the Vallandinghams were from New Albany, Indiana. Wally took that personally—which is precisely how Kentuckians, on the whole, take their basketball.

Clark made this clear one afternoon in late September as he sat, alone until approached, in the top row of the Coliseum's lower level watching the Kentucky players scrimmage informally. He had been doing this every day around 3:00, which gave him an advantage over Pitino, who wasn't allowed to watch until practice officially started on October 15. Through his studied observations, Clark had come to admire the defensive presence of Magloire around the basket, and he was the first to assure everyone that Jared Prickett, the big senior forward, was back strong after his injury and redshirt season. He marveled at Mercer and Anderson and got excited watching Jeff Sheppard go head-to-head with his counterpart from modern Kentucky history, former Wildcats idol Rex Chapman, now of the Phoenix Suns. He complained that Anthony Epps, the point guard, wore his drawers too low. He reflected wistfully on the days, 30 years ago, when he and other boys from the neighborhood shot baskets on that very floor with Louie Dampier and Pat Riley, and on being run out of there by the Baron himself, who he easily forgave. He remembered parking cars in his yard at Rose and Clifton: a dollar for the front yard and two for the back. He predicted, true to the color of his shirt, that the Cats would win it all again this year, but that the season—if not this, surely the next—would bring inevitable sadness, as well: Dean Smith of North Carolina was 25 victories from Rupp's all-time record of 876. Because of that, Clark had it in for Smith. It had become personal, just as it was, for him, with the Vallandinghams.

His feelings concerning the Vallandinghams were personal enough to become the driving force of his September and October. They were why he brushed his teeth every morning in the Coliseum bathroom. "They came from Indiana, and I wanted to beat 'em," Clark said. "I didn't set out to be in history. I just wanted to beat those people from Indiana. I hate Bobby Knight. I couldn't understand why we let somebody come from out of state and be the first person in line. They were first four out of five years. What I'd like to do is make it five in a row." This year was Clark's second. Last October he plopped down his lawn chair 17 days before the windows opened. The extra three weeks this year were insurance. "I don't think nobody else is gonna be that damn crazy," he said.

In 1985 the *Lexington Herald-Leader* printed an explosive series of articles about alleged improprieties in the Kentucky basketball program—payoffs and the like—for which the paper won a Pulitzer Prize. The series was so good, in fact, that subscriptions were canceled by the thousands. One man who called in to cancel was told that he didn't have a subscription. "Cancel it anyway," he grumbled. Bomb threats were phoned into the *Herald-Leader* offices and death threats delivered to the reporters. Street-corner vending boxes were shot up. A paperboy was run off a subscriber's property with an ax handle. Meanwhile, as the newspaper was losing favor and subscribers, there was no counter-balancing movement to turn in season tickets. Pressed to choose between investigative journalism and the Big Blue, most Kentuckians were not even conflicted. In an informal survey of 47 Lexingtonians, not one believed that the *Herald-Leader* series was justified. The provincial sentiment was summed up by an erstwhile reader who wrote a letter to the editor and signed it "Blue Bleeder." Concluding his passionate screed, Blue Bleeder heaped shame upon the editor for taking down Kentucky basketball, pointing out poignantly, "It's all we got."

To those who swear by it and seemingly live for it, Kentucky basketball is commonly characterized by the six NCAA championships the Wildcats have spread over 49 seasons, a chromatic half-century panorama featuring the enduring images of the Baron in his brown suit, Cliff Hagan's hook shot, Kyle Macy wiping his hands on his socks, Pitino's press, the nicknamed teams—the Fabulous Five, the Fiddlin' Five, Rupp's Runts, the Unforgettables—and perhaps most indelibly, the mountain family gathered around the wood stove, lost in the wintry radio voice of Cawood Ledford. So fundamental is Kentucky basketball to Kentucky culture that the commonwealth virtually shuts down on game night. When a teenaged driver in Harlan County swerved to avoid hitting a dog last year and struck a utility pole, knocking out power for Lorall and Baxter just as a UK game was about to come on television, the investigating officer refused to divulge the boy's name for fear of what some of the more enthusiastic viewers might do to him. In Kentucky the idea is not to let life interfere with basketball. Kentucky weddings are planned around the basketball schedule. The messiest part of a Kentucky divorce is custody of the season tickets. Kentucky caskets are available in blue and white. After the Macy-led team won the NCAA title in 1978, there was an outbreak of Kentucky babies named Kyle.

All of those things, though fanciful and revealing, do not adequately convey the depth of Kentucky's passion for basketball. They don't get to the heart of what makes Kentucky unique. Multiple championships have also been won at the likes of Indiana and Kansas and UCLA and Duke and North Carolina, among others, and basketball is very, very important to those places, as well. What's different about Kentucky is the way it reacted to the *Herald-Leader* series; the way the Kentucky fans bombarded the editors of *Street & Smith* last year when the magazine was so disrespectful as to place the Wildcats second in its preseason rankings; the way the Kentucky fans rose up in outrage in December 1983 when the Wildcats made a rare visit to Cincinnati (a Kentucky stronghold and a place where UK followers could actually get tickets) and the home team's overmatched coach devised a slowdown strategy, holding the score down and depriving the Big Blue folks of the massacre they had hungrily hoped to see; the way the Kentucky fans buried the sports department of *The* (Cincinnati) *Enquirer* with vitriolic mail, in record volume, after a columnist suggested that the '78 national champions were thugs; the way the Kentucky fans stood defiantly by their program after various violations (including the infamous Emery Worldwide money package involved in the recruitment of Chris Mills and other misdeeds of the nature that the *Herald-Leader* reported four years earlier) put it on a two-year probation in 1989; the way the Kentucky fans stirred up a running, front-page controversy last year when the Cats changed the shade of blue on their uniforms.

What distinguishes Kentucky from everywhere else is that basketball there seems to have family implications, as if every Kentuckian's good name is on the line. It is defended, accordingly, like a mother's virtue. Ask the natives why they feel that way about the university team and they'll say something about Adolph Rupp, something about tradition, and finally, invariably, they will say, "It's all we got." It's the one thing that's there for them when the national figures come out on education, when the coal mines close, when somebody makes another hillbilly joke. No one can make fun of Kentucky basketball, and pity the one who tries. The world can be cruel to Kentucky. Through basketball, Kentucky can get even.

Kentuckians realized this when Rupp started taking his mountain boys out of the South and whuppin' the big-city Northern teams. Before Rupp arrived in the fall of 1930, Kentucky basketball was a popular but still provincial thing. Rupp's predecessor at UK, John Mauer, had won the great majority of his games in three years but hadn't brought home a Southern Conference tournament title or beaten a big-time Eastern school. Consequently, the highlight of the commonwealth's basketball history was the 1928 state high school championship game, when Ashland and little Carr Creek struggled through four overtimes.

Before consolidation reduced the number of Kentucky high schools by nearly half, every two-mule community had one, and those with five boys had basketball teams. The Louisville and Lexington schools dominated the state tournaments early on, but that didn't keep the little teams from dreaming, and in 1928 along came Carr Creek. Perched on a mountain ledge in Knott County, Carr Creek High School educated 15 students, eight of them boys. There were baskets in the auditorium, but the ceiling wasn't high enough to accommodate full-fledged basketball, so they brought in the mules to level out a spot, tacked one goal on a chicken shed and the other on a railroad tie. The mountain dropped off about a hundred feet at the side of the court, which made skillful ball handlers of the Creekers, a talent that took them all the way to the state tournament, in which they appeared in uniforms bought for them by admiring fans of Richmond, where the regional was held.

That Ashland prevailed in the final game, 13–11, did little to diminish Carr Creek's legend, especially when Ashland went on to Chicago and won the national high school tournament. Before being swallowed up by consolidation, the Creekers would return to the state tournament (which pits schools of all sizes against each other) in 1956 and win it, climaxing a stretch of 17 years in which mountain schools claimed seven state championships.

Through Carr Creek's example at the state level and Ashland's at the national, rural Kentuckians had begun to appreciate the esteem that could come their way through basketball. And in that light, they would soon and profoundly come to appreciate the confident Kansas man who, arriving from an Illinois high school, declared himself the best damn coach in the country. Long before he was the winningest coach in college history, Adolph Rupp made a state feel good about itself.

"He's the one who put 'em on the map," says Rupp's only child, Herky, a tall, gentle Lexington cattleman who played for his father and later coached high school basketball in Kentucky. "He's the one who took 'em to New York to play the NYUs and the Holy Crosses, the ones that everybody across the nation had heard of because they were big-city teams. He's the one who took 'em to Chicago to play Illinois and Northwestern, and then on the train to South Bend for Notre Dame. When they beat those teams, it was something local people could stick their chest out about and say, 'Hey, that's us. We're better than you,' because Daddy's team had 'Kentucky' across their uniforms. It was the same thing as Carr Creek coming to Lexington. It was the state coming together and saying 'Look at us. We're a bunch of kids from all these small places, and that's us going up there and beating all these big-city kids.'"

As Rupp's teams gained in stature, and his fans in self-esteem, there developed in Kentucky a deep-seated, personal pride in UK basketball that might be construed as intercollegiate jingoism. The accumulating facts only bolstered this attitude. In 1946–47, the Southeastern Conference first team—chosen by performance in the league tournament—was made up entirely of UK players from the state of Kentucky (Wildcats All-American center Alex Groza, an Ohioan, played sparingly in the tourney because of back trouble and was relegated to the second team). After the Wildcats won their first NCAA championship in 1948, state pride expanded into nationalism as the Fabulous Five joined the AAU champion Phillips Oilers to win an Olympic gold medal in London.

The Wildcats repeated as national champions in 1949 and won again in 1951 with teams that would later be tainted by the Kentucky point-shaving scandal. The New York judge in that case entered a damning assessment of Rupp and his program, but Kentuckians expected no less from a New York judge. To them, the opinion was another example of down-home Kentucky being castigated by the haughty big-city East. The university president absolved Rupp, calling him "an honorable man who did not knowingly violate athletic rules." To do otherwise would have been to incur the type of reaction the *Herald-Leader* experienced in a later, more civilized day.

Much of Kentucky's illustrious basketball history, it seems, has been characterized by scandals being answered. It is something the Wildcats have done famously well over the generations. Five years after its 1952–53 season was wiped out by the point-shaving episodes, Kentucky won the national championship. Pitino was hired amid the rubble of the most recent probation, and in his seventh season the program was once again at the summit.

Being a basketball historian and a confident man, Pitino knew, of course, that he could take it there. Otherwise, he wouldn't have left the New York Knicks. But that was about all he knew for sure about Kentucky basketball. He had heard, of course, that the state was crazy about the game.

"Where I come from," he said last week in his Memorial Coliseum office at the end of the upper concourse, "being a basketball nut meant going to the gym and playing, studying the game, that sort of thing. Nothing like this." He caught a glimpse of his new world the night the coliseum filled up for his first Midnight Madness at Kentucky. When he staged the same sort of exhibition in his first year at Boston University, a crowd of 14 had shown up, most of them relatives of coaches and players. "I think that now, finally, I do have a full appreciation of the way Kentucky feels about basketball. But it has taken eight years."

Pitino has tried to explain the Kentucky phenomenon to his friends in New York, and he can't any more than he could explain Wally Clark to them. "People looking at Kentucky from the outside might say that's bizarre behavior, they're crazy," he said, reaching into his desk drawer for a picture of a cat watching a UK game. "No, it's not crazy. That's them. You've got to respect them for what and who they are. Or, if it's a situation where it involves somebody very old or somebody dying, you have to do what you can to accommodate them. That could mean bringing them to practice, getting them seats to a game or maybe a spot on the bench, or calling them. A lot of these people, their last wish has to do with Kentucky basketball.

"I got a letter from a woman whose husband died in a Kentucky warm-up suit. We get hundreds of letters like that and a lot of them have to do with dying. Another one came not long ago about a man who has a glass eye with *UK* etched into it. We also get a lot of children named for ex-ballplayers here. I have a dog named for me. I get a picture and a letter from the dog every now and then."

The fact is, Pitino could get almost anything in the state named for him these days. After restoring glory and honor to the Kentucky program, he has become both the savior and master of the land that Rupp built. "There are ups and downs to that," he said on the day after a controversy broke out over his appearance with President Clinton in Lexington, it having been previously reported that the coach was a Republican. The downs are things like that and not being able to go to restaurants. The ups, however, are so compelling—Pitino has no doubt, for instance, that private money could be raised in a heartbeat for the new arena he believes "this corporation called Kentucky basketball" unquestionably needs—that a street-raised New York Italian gym rat rejected a stupid-rich deal with the New Jersey Nets to stay in horse and tobacco land. The stuff on the other side of the fence might be greener, Pitino realizes, but the bluegrass has its advantages. "There's only one act in Kentucky," he says. "I think that's what sets us apart from other places."

It is also what has lavished upon him a regional fame that is disproportionate in size to the water in which he swims. As a native of America's biggest pond, Pitino sometimes feels the banks of the commonwealth closing in on him. "But," he points out—and to him, this is the thing that counts—"I love being the basketball coach at Kentucky."

Friday was freezing. A wicked turn came over the atmosphere Thursday night, pushing the Kentucky campers deeper into their sleeping bags. David Lewis arrived with his young son around 2:00 AM but couldn't get out of the car because of the rain and lightning. The temperature bottomed out in the 30s.

But even in the cold and wind, Friday was a festival. The ticket window would open at 6:00 PM, and that tingling prospect was enough to surmount the weather. At the front of the line, Wally Clark came and went with impunity—nobody would challenge his place on the 39th day—but the others in his vicinity hung close with respect to their purpose. There were Jim and Betty Ryle of Park Hills, who will soon be putting up their six-foot Christmas tree decorated with nothing but UK ornaments. In his spare time, Jim makes custom UK golf clubs.

There was recently married John Matthews, who has seen only one Kentucky game in his life, a loss to Mississippi State in 1962, despite the efforts of the great Cotton Nash. Matthews made a pact with his fiancée in October 1995: if the Cats won the NCAA, they would go ahead and get married after the season. He wanted to renege halfway through and do the deed regardless, but Kathy said a deal was a deal. The wedding was on September 6, in honor of UK's six national championships. He wore Converse basketball shoes. The wedding cake was a duplicate of Rupp Arena. Pitino sent a bottle of champagne. As other fans gathered around in admiration Friday afternoon, Matthews showed off his wedding ring: five sapphires, to represent the previous championships, and a diamond in the middle for 1996.

And there was a young northern Kentuckian named Jason Ryan, who said he wants the UK fight song to be played when he is buried in a UK casket. Hearing that, Mickey Brady, a 17-year veteran of the Madness line, approached excitedly and informed him that there's a company now offering that item as part of its standard inventory.

Ryan took vacation to arrive at Big Blue Madness two days in advance. It was good therapy for him. A few days before he left, his UK room—virtually everybody in the line has a UK room at home, with pictures and scrapbooks and the like—was broken into and, along with the stereo, the thieves took his *Sports Illustrated* commemorative issue signed by Tony Delk. But they didn't get his taco. After the Florida game last year, Ryan was hanging around Rupp Arena for Pitino's radio show and noticed that Pitino, who did commercials for Taco Bell, wasn't interested in the taco that somebody handed him, pointing out that it wasn't a double-decker. From the crowd, Ryan piped up and said he'd take it. At home, he placed the taco in a Ziploc bag and stashed it in the freezer.

On the occasion of the UMass game in the Final Four last year, Ryan ate blue food all day. His wife supplied the coloring. She indulges him. She didn't even complain when he brought their baby daughter home from the hospital in a UK jogging suit.

As they chatted away the hours until they could catch their first glimpse of this year's team, none of Ryan's temporary neighbors thought him unusual in the least, nor he them. They're merely Kentuckians.

"This is all we got," Ryan explained, shrugging. "Horses, tobacco, and UK basketball."

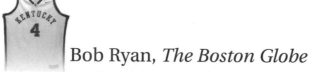

Bob Ryan, *The Boston Globe*

UK PROGRAM CARRIES WEIGHT OF A STATE ON ITS SHOULDERS

While covering the 1996 Final Four, legendary Boston Globe *reporter Bob Ryan takes a stab at trying to describe the aura, and pressure, surrounding the Big Blue.*

There is no other program like the Kentucky program. Players coming in think they understand this, but they only do so in the abstract. After a few years in the midst of the madness, they have a different perspective.

The Kentucky players were not just playing for themselves, their coach, and even their school when they took the floor against Syracuse last night for the 1996 NCAA championship. They were playing for untold thousands (conservative estimate) of people for whom each day without a Wildcat basketball game is a thoroughly wasted 24 hours.

"Where else could a player get between 100 and 200 letters a week from fans?" Kyle Macy once inquired. "Where else can a player have babies named after him?"

"You can be walking in a mall," says senior Walter McCarty, "and someone walks up, touches you, and starts screaming, 'I touched him!' It could be an old woman, 80 years old, trying to get your autograph. A lot of people go to extremes."

Joe B. Hall had both hands on this tiger's tail for 13 years. He had the frightening burden of succeeding the legendary Adolph Rupp, and so bad was the pressure in his day that his best team, the 1978 national champions, was widely recognized as the most joyless group of titlists in NCAA history. Neither he nor his players were allowed to enjoy themselves en route to the title, so foreboding was the Fear of Failure, a shortcoming that would have drawn the wrath of the entire commonwealth.

"They are so interested and intent in their following of the Wildcats that it makes for a very peculiar type of program," he said in a 1981 biography. "It's one in which everything the players do, both good and bad, is magnified. It is an awesome responsibility on a young man to be put in that position to where he can make or break himself by his actions on and off the court."

A Kentucky player takes an enormous gamble with his life. He bets that he can live up to the stringent demands of a great coach, and he bets that he can function as an animal in one of the American athletic world's strangest zoos.

The basketball part is difficult, but at least the major problems occur behind closed doors, when a player's imperfect game is stripped naked by Coach Rick Pitino. The live-up-to-the-image problems, the keep-the-customers-satisfied problems, and the everybody-knows-your-business problems might he harder for young people to handle than mere matters of athletics.

McCarty is from Indiana, which is not exactly basketball Siberia. But he comes from Evansville, which is close enough to the Kentucky border that McCarty figured he had some sense of the power Kentucky basketball holds over its citizenry.

"In Indiana, you've got IU [Indiana University] and Purdue, and in my hometown there is Evansville, but there's nothing like Kentucky. It's pretty much divided in Indiana. When you get to Kentucky and become a part of this university and its tradition, you learn what fan support is all about. Other places have fan support, but I don't think they go out on a limb as much as here."

McCarty no doubt could relate to the tale of Simeon J. Hale, who lived in a rural part of the state and who was in love with Wildcat basketball. He would walk from his (deep) country abode to a road where he would catch a bus to Somerset. There he would board another bus to Lexington. He would nap in the bus station until it was time to go to the game. After the game he would walk back to the station and sleep there until 3:00 AM, when the bus departed back to Somerset. Then he'd walk home. It would be a 24-hour ordeal. Simeon J. Hale made his last trip to Lexington at age 91.

Rick Pitino isn't 91 yet—he only feels that way if his team is trailing at halftime. He was far from naïve. He certainly knew what to expect when he took the Kentucky job. In fact, it's a good thing he did take the Kentucky job, because the list of those who are man enough for the task is practically as short as the compilation of Cecil Fielder's Most Memorable Stolen Bases.

"That job," observes Syracuse mentor Jim Boeheim, "has always been a monster. It's a basketball-crazed state. Rick might be the only modern coach who can handle that job for any length of time."

Even Pitino wasn't fully aware of the insanity. The epiphany came the first time someone showed up at the construction site of his new house to scoop up a sample of the dirt for a memento. Right then and there he understood that there were high-profile jobs and there was Kentucky.

"Sure, there's pressure," says Pitino, "but we try to make it a good pressure. We try to use it to inspire us to jump higher or run faster or shoot better."

Mike Littwin, *Los Angeles Times*

IN THE BLUEGRASS STATE, THEY'RE THOROUGHLY BRED TO WIN, OR ELSE

A West Coast view of Kentucky basketball madness, written during the 1981 season.

Here in the bluegrass, where the basketball rocks and the hills roll, only three things truly matter: horses, bourbon, and basketball.

Try to put them in any order and you risk a fight.

They breed horses here, the best horses. At Keeneland, site of the famed auction, some yearlings, such as the son of Secretariat, who lives nearby, sell for $1 million and more. Kentucky bourbon? Is there any finer? At Keeneland, during the auction, you'll find Kentucky gentlemen sipping that bourbon and talking basketball. University of Kentucky basketball.

Basketball wasn't invented here, but some claim it was perfected under the guiding hand of Adolph Rupp, at Kentucky.

It's a place where tickets are so scarce (in a 23,000-seat arena) that a body might trade one of those horses for two at midcourt.

Where a bumper sticker was seen that read: "A Kentucky pervert: someone who likes sex more than basketball."

Where there's a tabloid, the Cat's Pause, that sells 23,000 copies a week of 32 pages or more about Kentucky basketball.

Rupp migrated here from Kansas 50 years ago, and the Wildcats have hardly missed a beat since, not even when Joe B. Hall succeeded the legendary Rupp (down here you get the impression *legendary* was his first name) nine years ago.

Five NCAA championships, 32 in the Southeastern conference, two more from the NIT. The press guide, which prints the Wildcats' losses in boldface type they're so rare, lists the 1948 team as *world* champions. Seems five Wildcats were on the gold-medal Olympic team that year.

Good is one thing. UCLA's been good. Better than Kentucky over the last few decades, in fact. But Bruin basketball is not a religion. It has trouble passing for a mania. But in Kentucky...

The Wildcats play three preseason scrimmages, one apiece in the eastern, central, and western parts of the state. All sell out, these scrimmages. At the one in Marshall County High in the western part of the state, scalpers were getting as much as $60 for a $10 ticket.

The morning of the Notre Dame game in Louisville, 12,000 showed up to watch the team practice.

In Lexington, where the beautiful new Rupp Arena's 23,000 seats were supposed to end ticket headaches, every regulation game since 1963 has been a sellout. An exhibition against the South Koreans this year drew 18,200. Student tickets are sold on Sunday for the next week's games. Lines begin to form on Friday.

You should be getting the picture by now. Only it's so large that no canvas could do it justice.

Even though it starts four sophomores, Kentucky rated number one in preseason polls because it's Kentucky. The Wildcats hit the skids recently, losing two straight. Panic began to set in, because it's Kentucky. You have to understand, it was the Wildcats' worst slump in three years.

The Tradition

Dirk Minniefield is a mere sophomore at Kentucky. Maybe "mere" is the wrong word. As the point guard for the basketball team, he's a bona fide celebrity, as all Kentucky basketball players are in varying degrees. Talk about your idols, you can actually buy statues of some of them. He's also a heads-up young man with more than a clue about what's going on around him.

"The tradition here hangs over Coach Hall's head like a hammer," Minniefield says.

So it does. Like Thor's, the hammer is primed to crash down at any time. On Hall. On Minniefield. On any basketball-playing unfortunate who risks the wrath of the gods. It hangs above them all. But it is to Hall that the mantle was passed, and he thinks he wears it well enough.

Some others aren't always certain. It isn't that long ago that the Baron, Adolph Rupp, retired, against his will. And not that long since he died. There are some, to this day, surprised that either could have happened. Not much ever happened around here that the Baron hadn't approved.

Kentucky Fan, Player, Coach

He took over the program in 1930 and left it 42 years and 880 victories later. He was irascible, controversial, and a legend. He brought basketball with him from Kansas and introduced it to the South. He took his Southern team North and played in Noo Yawk and beat the Yankees at their own game. He won championships and he made this school, this town, his barony. He chased off Bear Bryant, who was for a while football coach at Kentucky, and forced him to become a legend elsewhere.

Joe B. Hall probably will never be called a baron, or a legend, or anything close to either. That doesn't seem to bother him. He grew up a Kentucky fan, played at Kentucky, was Rupp's longtime assistant and eventually his successor. And although Rupp's mind became poisoned against Hall in the end, Hall says he had only love for Adolph.

"Being compared, and nearly always in unfavorable circumstances, with Rupp never bothered me," Hall says. "It was like following your father. I respect his records. I kind of want him to have them always."

So would Rupp, most likely. There are plenty still around who remember him well enough, but maybe none better than Harry Lancaster, who was his assistant for 25 years and later Kentucky athletics director. He's retired now but serves as a volunteer coach, pretty much an honorary position.

"Adolph and Joe were very different," Lancaster says. "Adolph was good copy, a writer's dream. He'd think of controversial things to say. He was colorful and liked attention. Joe is low profile. He doesn't need attention."

Hall Is No Rupp

"But Joe does a good job," says Lancaster. "He's got a good program, one that Kentucky can be proud of."

It is a good program, maybe even good enough. But Hall is not Rupp and never can be, which is why Kentucky basketball, be it bigger than ever, can never quite be what it was.

"Adolph didn't really have to recruit," Lancaster says. "He'd send me up into the hills [in Eastern Kentucky] to see some big old boy [always white] who was living in some cabin with hogs running around in the front yard. I'd take 'em down to see Adolph, and that was that. Give them a warm bed and three hot meals a day and they thought you'd given them the world.

"Adolph used to say: 'I lift up mine eyes unto the hills from whence comes my salvation.'"

And he'd whip those hillbillies and Kentucky farm boys—there were no black players until the '70s—into shape, Rupp style. He was tough, very tough. Some of the stories are legend. Like the time he asked one of his players, one who hadn't lived up to his promise, if he wanted to be remembered at Kentucky. When the player nodded yes, Rupp roared: "Then you'd better go rape the dean of women because that's the only way."

Lancaster tells of Frank Ramsay who, one day in practice, was advised by Rupp that there must be insanity in his family. "Frank came to me in tears," Lancaster says, "and said he did have one aunt who was slightly off, but how could Coach Rupp know about her."

There were Rupp's Runts and the Fabulous Five and all the championship teams. But in the end, when Rupp, nearly blind and some say nearly senile as well, wouldn't let go, he was forced out. Mandatory retirement was invoked. And Hall, who had left briefly to be coach at St. Louis only to be called back and promised the Kentucky job if he would stay, was to be the successor.

"Didn't Want to Leave"

"Adolph didn't want Hall," Lancaster says. "He became suspicious of him."

"It hurt me," Hall says, "but I know he would have been the same with anyone. He just didn't want to leave."

Rupp spent his last days in a made-up job as a vice president of the Kentucky Colonels of the American Baseball Association, a bitter man. But he had left his legacy, if not his blessing, for Hall.

It was as Rupp was fond of saying: "When a Kentucky baby is born, the mother naturally wants him to grow up to be president, like another Kentuckian, Abraham Lincoln. If not president, she wants him to play basketball at the University of Kentucky."

The Coach

Perhaps the best description of Joe B. Hall came from Joe B. Hall himself. "I've been called," he says, "simple looking, simple named, simple dressed, simple speaking—everything but simpleminded— and somebody probably said that too, just not to my face."

If the description is, uh, simplistic, it is also not without grains, maybe chunks, of truth. Hall's a slick enough country boy, but hardly slick looking. He's got short hair and a paunch. His clothes won't be mistaken for designer brand, except by those who confuse J.C. Penny with Yves St. Laurent. Hall might.

If clothes don't make this man, his style of coaching does. He's tough, a disciplinarian. Said Sam Bowie, his 7'1" sophomore star: "Not everyone can play for him. You have to understand that you're going to do things his way, period. You have to be able to handle his screaming. I can. I'm used to it."

Hall suspends star players (Bowie was one) before crucial games for what some might consider minor offenses—say a missed curfew. He's hard to play for, demanding. A lot of players transfer, but a lot more stay, and for the last two years Hall has had as good a group of recruits as any school in the country.

He's a salesman above all, even convincing the tough Kentucky fans, so many of whom were against him at the start, that he's their kind of coach. Winning the NCAA title in '78 didn't hurt. But he didn't hurt himself either.

"Coach Rupp would have his secretary throw out all the hate mail," Hall said. "I want mine. I read each letter and answer each one. They tear me up, tell me what a lousy job I'm doing. And I sit down and write them a letter, tell them they're entitled to their opinion, and even point out where I might agree with them."

Hall has taken abuse and given out little except to his players and an occasional sportswriter. It's a successful formula. But Hall has been preparing all his life for this job, even before he realized it. He grew up in Cynthiana, a Kentucky town 60 miles from Lexington, hoping to be a football player. Which meant, even more so in those days, that he hoped to play for Notre Dame. He also grew up a Kentucky basketball fan and, after trying out—you did that in those days, too—would play for Adolph Rupp.

Unable to break into Kentucky's starting lineup, Hall transferred, with Rupp's aid and blessing, to Sewanee, where he set scoring records. Upon graduation, he toured Europe with a team that played preliminary games ahead of the Globetrotters in the summer of '51. He remembers that time as "the most exciting of my life." He settled down to be a high school coach and thought he'd end his days there.

Replacing Wooden Tougher

But he went on to coach at Regis College in Colorado and Central Missouri State until Rupp called him home to Kentucky.

He says that succeeding Rupp was not as difficult for him as succeeding John Wooden at UCLA was for Gene Bartow. The circumstances were comparable but, according to Hall (who once joked that he was the best candidate for the UCLA job, saying, "Why ruin two lives?"), also different.

"I knew the program," he said. "I knew everything about it, from every vantage point. I knew it as a fan, as a player, and as an assistant coach. There were no surprises. It was just what I expected it to be."

He took over nine years, one NCAA championship, and 192 wins ago. When in his first season Kentucky lost its first home opener in a decade, disaffection began to set in. But he led Kentucky to the league title and was SEC Coach of the Year. It was a start. But in his next year, Kentucky, which hasn't had a losing record since 1927, was 13–13, and some were hoping that he would be finished. But Hall's a survivor, strong enough to hold his ground.

"I don't have an ego problem," he says. "I don't need to be famous. Being famous is more of a hindrance than anything else. I don't break in lines or get good tables at a restaurant because I'm Joe B. Hall. I can take criticism. I understand it. I don't always like it, but I can live with it."

Own Brand of Discipline

"Winning is an obsession at Kentucky," says Hall. "That's not a bad thing. It keeps you on your toes. I feel we have to win here. And I don't doubt for a moment we have a winning program. That doesn't mean you have to win a national championship every year, but you have to be a contender. You have to be able to honestly say, at any time, that within two years you'll be contending for the NCAA title."

Hall has done that here. He's done it with his own brand of discipline, a scowl on his face, and enough talent to start his own agency.

But he hasn't gotten popular doing it. His press isn't particularly good. He doesn't go out of his way to make a good impression, but that's not to say he agrees with the impression most people have of him.

"I'm much softer than my image," Hall says. "People think I'm all serious, all business, all hard-nosed, no fun. That's ridiculous."

The System

Kentucky basketball players live in the Joe B. Hall Wildcat Lodge. It deserves four stars by any hotel rating. Once it would have gotten five, but NCAA investigators, picky types, made Kentucky move out the seven-foot beds and big-screen TVs and said that other students—real students—had to live there, too.

Hall raised the money, about $750,000, for the lodge himself. Joked Harry Lancaster: "If Adolph thought he could have raised that kind of money, he'd have done it and bought himself a farm."

Hall's a farm boy, too, but having toured Europe, he knows something about castles. And if UK basketball players can't pass as royalty here in the bluegrass, just who can?

That's part of the system—plushness, privilege. Pressure is also part of the system, an insistence on excellence. And discipline is a part, Joe B. Hall style.

Players Videotaped

"Coach Hall is always yelling at you," sophomore Minniefield says, "telling you about the tradition here and how you have to uphold it. Fans get down on you too, even if you win but don't play well. That might not be fair somewhere else, but it is here because you know what's come before."

There's more to being a Kentucky basketball player than dribbling and dunking a basketball; more even than winning games and championships.

The speech and drama department at Kentucky videotapes interviews with the players, intent on removing the "uhs" and "you knows." So Kentucky players talk right. The home economics department gives the players lessons in manners. "Most of these youngsters," Hall says, "have never eaten with three forks unless they had dropped two on the floor." So Kentucky players act right. It's all part of an image, one that Hall believes is required and to which the players don't object, at least not aloud.

"Kentucky is different than most programs because the players live a fishbowl existence," Hall says. "You have to have discipline. Our program would destroy itself without discipline. The atmosphere and morality around Lexington demand it. If we didn't have it, we wouldn't have the support of people whose support we need.

"It doesn't hurt to have your hair short. It doesn't hurt to have good manners. It doesn't hurt to speak well and look good... They'll look like better people, even if they're not."

Molded His Own Team

All part of the system. Hall initiated a weight program, once scorned by basketball minds but now an accepted and growing practice, and produced Wildcats that resembled lions. They're big and physical. That's part of Kentucky basketball. So are long and difficult practices, which run like clockwork, almost football style. Hall's favorite punishment for a player who blows an assignment in practice is to have him "hit the wall," meaning climb the steps to the top of the arena. In the practice gym, that's tough enough. In giant Rupp Arena, you hit the wall.

Hall, then, has molded his team according to his personal principles. Some people say Kentucky basketball players have no fun. But senior Fred Cowan, for one, said: "Winning is fun." Even with the discipline.

"What's difficult," Hall said, "is to discipline without over-disciplining. It's reasonable to bench a kid for missing a curfew. What's not reasonable, but unavoidable, is the headlines the punishment gets. I can punish my own kids in the privacy of my home without the neighbors knowing about it. But you have to explain to people why one of their heroes won't play that night."

The Star

Sam Bowie is a marvel. He's 7'1" and, thanks to Hall's weight program, a nearly sturdy 235 pounds. He can dribble the ball behind his back. He can shoot a legitimate 20-foot jumper. He's 19 and tall, an often awkward combination, but Bowie is as smooth as good Kentucky whiskey. He plays tennis. He used to dive into pools until Hall figured he'd just as soon not have the floor of his pool spoiled by contact with Bowie's head. Bowie's bright and likes to talk about the importance of a degree and what classes mean to him. He's well-mannered, a good interview. Almost too good to be true.

Oh, he's a marvel all right. Maybe too marvelous.

The problem with Sam Bowie is that he hasn't quite got it into his head what a 7'1" center, especially one with his agility and jumping ability, should be.

"He's not that aggressive," Hall said. "He's not an intimidator. He's getting better at it, but it's not something you can easily teach."

Bowie understands the problem, of course. "My heart's on the outside," he says, "but my future's on the inside."

He'd like to be a guard, or a forward. He tried to persuade Ralph Sampson, the 7'4" sophomore center for Virginia, to accompany him to Kentucky so Sampson could play the low post and Bowie away from the basket.

Inside or out, he's wonderful. His potential greatness is not at question. It's a matter of degrees.

A sophomore on a team of freshman and sophomore stars, Bowie is the stuff of which championships are made. He's also the stuff of interviews and fan adulation and lack of privacy.

"I feel a little guilty about all the attention," he says. "I don't know how I'd feel if it was someone else."

Says Dirk Minniefield: "We don't mind because if someone comes to look at Sam, he sees us too."

He's been a celebrity since his high school days in Lebanon, a steel-mill town in eastern Pennsylvania. When he led his high school to the state championship his junior year, Lebanon celebrated with a parade. Next thing you know, there were Sam Bowie posters and Sam Bowie buttons and Sam Bowie T-shirts.

Bowie didn't know what to make of it all. Still doesn't. "I go home now," he says, "and people are fantasizing about me. I can't just be one of the guys anymore."

Played on Olympic Team

It happens he's one of the best guys around in short pants, considerably better than he was last year. "He's gotten more into the game," teammate Cowan said. "Sometimes he just takes over."

Playing on the U.S. Olympic team last year helped, especially banging heads and bodies with such NBA centers as Artis Gilmore and Bob Lanier. He's learned what it is to be pushed and what it is to push back. And, after playing against these bigger players, he has less trouble with the many defenses devised by college teams to stop him.

They lob him the ball inside or he takes the jumper outside or he's passing off the low post. Maybe blocking a shot. There's not much Bowie can't do.

But, somehow, it's not always enough. "We were 29–6 last year and there were people who thought it was an off season," he says. "Win or lose, the sun still shines the next day. When we lose, we didn't go into the game with the intention of losing. Other teams don't get any credit. Kentucky isn't supposed to lose."

The Team

Here it is January and the Wildcats have already lost three games. They've dropped as low as number five in the polls. LSU is probably going to win the SEC title. And Joe Hall is beside himself.

"I don't see how we could have been picked number one," he said. "We are so young, with eight freshmen and sophomores among our first 10 players."

Ah, but what freshmen and sophomores. The Bowie class may prove to be one of the best ever recruited at Kentucky. Bowie is the best of the lot, of course. The centerpiece. Every team that plays Kentucky comes to play Bowie first and then the rest of the team.

Minniefield is the sophomore point guard, solid with good quickness. He runs the offense well and can score. Bowie calls him "our spiritual leader." Derrick Hord is a 6'6" swingman, also a sophomore, playing the other guard position. Good scorer, another of the Kentucky strongmen. Stronger yet is 6'6" forward Charles Hurt, he of the spectacular slam dunks. The sophomore is playing in place of junior Chuck Verderber, who is out for another month following an appendectomy. Fred Cowan is a senior forward and team's second-leading scorer.

On the bench are four freshmen: shooter Jim Master, quick Dick Beal, 6'9" forward Brent Bearup, and 6'11" Melvin Turpin. They'd like Turpin, a strongman, to play alongside Bowie, reminiscent of the Kentucky championship teams that featured Rick Robey and Mike Phillips, both 6'11". So far, it hasn't worked too well.

"Inexperience," says Cowan, "is the only thing that can stop us from going all the way," All the way, in Kentuckyese, means NCAA championship. The Wildcats may be a little young to go all the way.

But they may get there. A good bunch of kids, Hall calls them. "Almost too good," he says.

"They do what you ask them to do by the letter," he says. "But they get mechanical. They don't seek and sense options. They try to be good team players, but they overdo it.

"They're very talented, but they're not playing hard enough, or with enough intensity."

Watching them dive for balls—even Bowie—and play that physical brand of Kentucky basketball, one had trouble questioning this team's intensity or desire. But they have lost a couple, and at Kentucky, like at UCLA, there must be a reason.

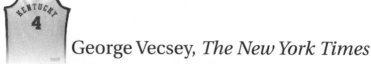

George Vecsey, *The New York Times*

THE WAR WITHIN THE STATE

Kentucky-Louisville isn't the oldest or most storied rivalry in college basketball, but because of the commonwealth's love of the game, it evokes as much emotion and passion as any series over the last 20 years. George Vecsey captured the series' history in this 1984 article.

When I was a news reporter in Kentucky in the early '70s, one of the first things I learned was the utter futility of doing business on basketball nights. It did no good to interview coal operators or farmers in their homes on basketball night because their eyes would keep darting to the television set and their answers were likely to be: "How about those Wildcats?" The same was true of politicians or activists in the big city of Louisville, except their response to the television was likely to be: "Look at those Cardinals."

It was clear to a visitor that the state that had been so bitterly divided from 1861 to 1865 was now divided over basketball. The University of Kentucky Wildcats were the darlings of almost the entire Commonwealth of Kentucky; the University of Louisville was loved mainly in a few square miles on the south side of the Ohio River.

The division may not be as one-sided as it seemed last night in Rupp Arena, where about 18,000 of the 23,000 fans seemed to be wearing apparel of Wildcat blue and rooting for UK against U of L in the National Collegiate Athletic Association Mideast Regional. Kentucky won, 72–67.

It took an NCAA pairing to get these two nonplaying rivals on the same court last year for the first time in 24 years. Then it took blatant public pressure to get Kentucky to schedule Louisville to a four-year series that began last November.

The disdain for Louisville is partly the reflection of Kentucky's pride in five national championships. When Louisville finally won the NCAA tournament in 1980, T-shirts appeared showing five Kentucky

Wildcats holding NCAA banners. The message on the T-shirt was: "And don't you forget it."

There's very little subtlety in basketball or politics, two of the main passions in Kentucky. I'll never forget the election I covered when the state changed hands and one party hack got up in front of a television camera and said: "They've had it for four years. Now it's our turn at the trough."

The rivalry has its roots in old political and social divisions. When Albert "Happy" Chandler made his numerous campaigns for Governor and Senator, he would gain votes by suggesting that Kentucky reroute the Ohio River and bequeath Louisville to Indiana.

The city of Louisville always seemed a little fast for the rest of the state. Then Louisville's basketball team was integrated long before Kentucky got around to it in 1971. Louisville's all-black starting team in 1980, the high-fiving doctors of dunk who won the national tournament, seemed to stiffen resistance in Lexington, where horse farms and brick mansions are the most northern outpost of the South.

Joe B. Hall, who took over as coach for Adolph Rupp in 1973, never liked being prodded to play Louisville. Certainly the Baron never had to put up with cheeky suggestions like that. Once Hall was asked about it in front of a television camera and his response was: "Cut, dissolve."

In 1982 Louisville and Kentucky were placed in the same NCAA regional bracket, and Derek Smith of Louisville said: "If there is a God, this will be the year these two schools will meet."

After speculators tried to buy up the scarce tickets—one man claimed to have paid $960 for four tickets at a deserted gas station in the middle of the night—Kentucky lost to Middle Tennessee in the first round.

But the NCAA persevered and put the two rivals in the same bracket again last year. This time they met in the regional final in Knoxville, Tennessee, and Louisville won, 80–68, in overtime. After decades of hand-wringing over potential violence, the game was peaceful as Louisville and Kentucky cheerleaders posed amicably in a mélange of red and blue. The most violent touch was the half-blue, half-red suit worn by John Y. Brown, the flamboyant governor of Kentucky.

Governor Brown, a graduate of UK who was nearing the end of his term and preparing for this year's run for the Senate, was a major supporter of a series between the two schools, an act that will not exactly hurt him in populous Louisville.

"We had nothing to gain," Cliff Hagan, the Kentucky athletics director, said yesterday. "If you're competing, you don't want to do anything that will help your competitor. There's a big fight for media attention. Louisville has had a fine program for 30 years. Neither of us needed this game, but the politicians got involved."

Nevertheless, Kentucky enjoyed every moment of last November's 65–44 thrashing of a young Louisville team, and so did people in Cynthiana and Greasy Creek and Monkey's Eyebrow and wherever else baskets are still hung on the sides of barns.

Hagan said that because of the two meetings in the past year, last night's game was just another Louisville-Kentucky game: "The blossom has been plucked."

With the great bulk of fans rooting for Kentucky, there was hardly the feeling of a "neutral site" for a national tournament.

Jim Master, the Kentucky guard, tried to downplay the home advantage by saying, "Really, it's a different atmosphere from a regular home game. The other teams' supporters root against us because we're the home team."

But Denny Crum, the Louisville coach, said, "Maybe a neutral site would have made a difference; I'll never know." He also knew his head hurt from a flying quarter that hit him from behind. Crum added: "I don't think a Louisville fan did it."

Let us close with an old Kentucky joke. A man is sitting in the top row at Rupp Arena and he notices an empty seat in the second row. He walks down and asks the woman if the seat is empty. She says it is. A few minutes later, he comments that it seems strange to see a vacant seat at Rupp. She says the seat used to belong to her husband, but he passed away.

"Well, surely there must be somebody else in the family who can use the ticket," the man says.

"Oh, they're all at the funeral," the woman replies.

NOTES

The publisher has made every effort to determine the copyright holder for each piece in *Echoes of Kentucky Basketball*.

Reprinted with permission of *The Washington Post*: "The Right Mixture of Love, Hate Kept Rupp on Top" by Dave Kindred, copyright © 1977 *The Washington Post*; "Book on Kentucky: Only Title Page Is Flawed" by John Feinstein, copyright © 1983 *The Washington Post*; "Hall's Light Touch Gives Kentucky Old Feeling" by Michael Wilbon, copyright © 1984 *The Washington Post*; "Counted Down and Out, Kentucky Injected with New Life by Pitino" by Scott Fowler, copyright © 1990 *The Washington Post*.

Reprinted with permission of *The New York Times*: "His Old Kentucky Home" by Arthur Daley (January 4, 1944), copyright © 1944 by The New York Times Co.; "Kentucky Defeats Baylor in NCAA Basketball Final at Garden" by Louis Effrat (March 24, 1948), copyright © 1948 by The New York Times Co.; "From Old Kaintuck" by Arthur Daley (December 17, 1948), copyright © 1948 by The New York Times Co.; "Kentucky's Baron Still Holding Court" by Gerald Eskenazi (March 14, 1976), copyright © 1976 by The New York Times Co.; "Kentucky Easily Beats Louisville, 65–44" by Peter Alfano (November 27, 1983), copyright © 1983 by The New York Times Co.; "The War within the State" by George Vecsey (March 23, 1984), copyright © 1984 by The New York Times Co.; "The Frustration Ends for Beal" by Malcolm Moran (March 26, 1984), copyright © 1984 by The New York Times Co.; "At Kentucky, Tradition Takes a Twist" by Timothy W. Smith (November 18, 1997), copyright © 1997 by The New York Times Co.; "Duke-Kentucky II: A Sequel to Remember" by William C. Rhoden (March 23, 1998), copyright © 1998 by The New York Times Co.; "Kentucky's Newton Has Come Full Circle" by William C. Rhoden (March 29, 1998), copyright © 1998 by The New York Times Co.

"Sky-High Kentucky Cuts Houston Down to Size" by Fred Mitchell, copyrighted 1/23/1984, Chicago Tribune Company. All rights reserved. Used with permission.

Reprinted courtesy of *The* (Cincinnati) *Enquirer*: "Firm Hands, Loving Hands" by Neil Schmidt, January 8, 2005.

Reprinted courtesy of *The Philadelphia Inquirer*: "Hatton Knots First Extra Set on 47-Footer" by Herb Good, December 8, 1957.

"Guard Powers Cats to Win Over Archrival" by Pat Forde © ESPN/ Starwave Partners d/b/a ESPN Internet Venture. Reprinted courtesy of ESPN.com.

Reprinted courtesy of the *Los Angeles Times*: "In the Bluegrass State, They're Thoroughly Bred to Win, or Else" by Mike Littwin, January 28, 1981; "The Comeback of Sam Bowie" by Jerry Crowe, December 23, 1983.

Reprinted courtesy of *The Sporting News*: "Beard Thinks, Eats, Lives Basketball" by Tommy Fitzgerald, December 22, 1948; "Rupp's Cats Fiddle Away" by Joe Gergen; "Macy's Magic" by Joel Bierig, January 19, 1980; "Chapman, Basketball Inseparable" by John McGill, January 25, 1988; "Mash Bash" by Michael Bradley, November 30, 1992.

Reprinted with permission of Orange Frazer Press: "Bleeding UK Big Blue" by Lonnie Wheeler. Originally published in *Blue Yonder: Kentucky: The United State of Basketball*.